Charting *the* Range *of* Black Politics

THE NATIONAL POLITICAL SCIENCE REVIEW

Charting *the* Range *of* Black Politics

National Political Science Review, Volume 14

Michael Mitchell
David Covin, *editors*

A Publication of the National Conference of Black Political Scientists

Transaction Publishers
New Brunswick (U.S.A.) and London (U.K.)

Library of Congress Catalog Number: 2012007988
ISBN: 978-1-4128-4939-5
Printed in the United States of America

Library of Congress Cataloging-in-Publication Data

Charting the range of Black politics / Michael Mitchell and David Covin, editors.
    p. cm. — (National political science review ; v. 14)
    ISBN 978-1-4128-4939-5
  1. African Americans—Politics and government—21st century. 2. Obama, Barack—Influence. 3. United States—Race relations—Political aspects. 4. United States—Politics and government—2009- I. Mitchell, Michael, 1944- II. Covin, David, 1940-
    E185.615.C5615 2012
    323.1196'0730905—dc23
                                                                2012007988

Contents

Editors' Note

Barack Obama's election to the presidency has prompted rethinking in the way that scholars have customarily mapped out the terrain of Black politics. President Obama has brought onto the national stage the complexities confronting the member of a minority group assuming power over national political institutions and the limits placed on that power by virtue of the double accountability such a figure faces, both from his own minority community as well as from the larger majority population. The question, therefore, arises: might the ascendancy of President Obama lead to a deracialization of American politics, or even its opposite? Either course remains open and continues to be the subject of serious discussion.

The contents in the current volume of the *National Political Science Review* in one way or another speak to this question. The "Articles" section draws on work presented at the 2011 meeting of the National Conference of Black Political Scientists. Among these works, the editors solicited contributions from David Wilson and Khalilah Brown-Dean of the University of Delaware and Yale University, respectively, who analyze Black attitudes toward the candidates for the Democratic Party nomination in the presidential race of 2008. Wilson and Brown-Dean found that a candidate's strategy of deemphasizing his racial identity and the salience of racial issues, in an effort to appeal to White voters, has the opposite and potentially negative effect on Black voters. Wilson's and Brown-Dean's work was the winner of the Best Paper Prize at the 2011 National Conference of Black Political Scientists meeting.

Michael Clemons assesses the impact of the racial factor in shaping public support for President Obama's foreign policy. Clemons observes that while there existed clear and long-standing differences between Blacks and Whites regarding foreign policy, Blacks appear to have become more favorably inclined to the Obama administration's foreign policy initiatives. Clemons attributes this shift to the generally favorable attitudes that Blacks show for Obama himself. Lorenzo Morris of Howard University continues this discussion of race and foreign policy. Morris asks how perceptions of race have defined the expectations held of the African American ambassadors to the United Nations. Morris has found that since the earliest of these ambassadors, starting with Ralph Bunch, race had played a significant part in perceptions of the kinds of policy emphasis Black ambassadors would place on their missions. Susan Rice, however, although she shares similar characteristics with President Obama, has become, arguably, the prototype of the "invisible diplomat."

The concerns of Black political scientists, as these articles illustrate, stretch beyond areas confined to domestic policy. One topic where an intersection of concerns occurs is the subject of the analysis by Horace Bartilow of the University of Kentucky and

Kihong Eom of Kyungpook University. Using a game theortic approach, Bartilow and Eom examine U.S. drug interdiction strategies in the Caribbean Basin. They bring a methodological freshness to a topic that cuts across both domestic and international concerns as well as one that draws a discussion of this sort closer to the diasporan links with the Caribbean region.

Two essays comprise the "Works in Progress" section. Two senior scholars, Michael C. Dawson of the University of Chicago and Andra Gillespe of Emory University, offer personal reflections on their work and the manner in which they assemble it. They follow in the tradition of C. Wright Mills in writing about intellectual craftsmanship, that is, of how their own personal concerns and curiosities guide the building of their research.

A "Book Review" section follows with an introduction by Tiffany Willoughby-Herard. These reviews provide an extended discussion from scholars and activists about the works of interest to the community of scholars committed to a dialogue on themes pertinent to the study of Black politics.

Articles

Great[er] Expectations:
The Double-Edged Sword of Deracialization

David C. Wilson and Khalilah L. Brown-Dean

Introduction

Group-based identities serve as a frequent and useful lens for filtering voters' evaluations of candidates and issues (Bobo 1988; Kuklinski and Quirk 2000; Popkin 1991). Similarly, political candidates often frame their issue priorities and presentation style to appeal to these identities and court particular constituencies (Neuman et al. 2007; Reeves 1997). The centrality of racial identification and identity in political judgments for African Americans is particularly well established (Dawson 1994; Tate 1994). African Americans use race as both a filter for political judgments (Glaser 1995) and as a basis for affective reactions to political figures (Tate 1994, 2003).

Though Black candidates also make use of racial heuristics, the existing literature suggests it can be a double-edged sword. Anecdotal evidence from both scholars and practitioners suggests that in order to win office in non-majority-minority districts, Black candidates may have to downplay racial group identities and attachments (Ifill 2009; Gillespie 2009). This argument centers on the idea of deracialization (McCormick and Jones 1993) which involves deliberate attempts to frame a candidate or campaign around race-neutral issues while avoiding explicit discussions related to race in order to win broader support among non-Black voters (McCormick and Jones 1993; Orey 2006; Wright-Austin and Middleton 2004; Wright 1995, 1996). While most of the literature examining deracilization focuses on the White electorate, there is scant evidence of how deracialization strategies might influence African American voters.

Prevailing theories (Mansbridge 1999; Reese and Brown 1995; Tate 1993, 2003) of group-based politics suggest that African Americans will prefer candidates who share their racial background over those candidates who do not. This argument commonly assumes racial loyalty trumps some sophisticated political calculus that takes into consideration the politics of the candidates. In other words, the common assumption is that being Black (i.e., racial similarity) is enough to ensure support in the African American electorate for Black candidates. Yet, there are prominent cases where Black candidates have not received broad support among African Americans.[1]

Critics contend that deracialization strategies devalue/undervalue African Americans and other underrepresented groups as important members of electoral coalitions (Pohlman and Kirby 1996) and risk alienating racial minorities (Orey 2006).[2] Some minority group members may view the rejection of their support at the electoral phase as an indication that their group's interests will also be overlooked once the candidate is elected to office. Thus, Black candidates can be doubly bound by their racial identity; constrained by the issues they can speak to *and* the expectations of different constituencies who will interpret their stance.

Among constituents who share their racial background, Black candidates are perhaps evaluated based on greater expectations: they have to simultaneously prove they are viable *and* able to provide substantive representation of racial group interests. A Black candidate that has problems resolving this tension will likely garner diffuse support among African Americans.

This tension between the need to appeal to White voters and the desire to shore up support among Black voters was highlighted in the pre-primary stages—circa the summer of 2007—of the 2008 presidential Democratic primary race.[3] Among African Americans the Democratic nomination was a two candidate competition between a White female candidate, Hillary Clinton, and a Black male candidate, Barack Obama (Newport et al. 2009). While issues of race were raised frequently during the latter stages of the 2008 primary, the early stages were a relatively benign period where race was less salient and candidates were gaining their policy footing.

We investigate whether African Americans liked *and* preferred Barack Obama simply because he was "Black," or whether voters' evaluations were based on a more sophisticated consideration of racial group interests.[4] Given the many claims that Barack Obama ran a deracialization campaign (Gillespie 2009), we evaluate the early part of his primary candidacy, rather than his election, as a case that is substantively and theoretically important for evaluating broader features of American political behavior in general, and Black political behavior in particular. Given the sporadic analyses of African American public opinion in American politics, and the dearth of empirical research on its role in ostensibly deracialized contests we focus mainly on their views.[5]

Deracialization as Electoral Strategy and Candidate Perception

Deracialization campaign strategies are guided by an explicit awareness of White voters' cautiousness, assessments of candidate viability, and assumptions that Black candidates will primarily advocate liberal and racial agendas (Citrin et al. 1990; Hajnal 2006; Hamilton 1977; Kaufmann 2008; McDermott 1998; McCormick and Jones 1993; Perry 1996; Reeves 1997; Wilson 2008). Deracialization candidates avoid using overt references to racial issues, public appeals to the Black community, and being associated with controversial racialized events or individuals (McCormick and Jones 1993).[6] These strategies have become common place as Blacks attempt to seek higher political office in majority White areas with little to no history of African American political leadership.

Candidates must also project a non-threatening or non-stereotypical political image (Citrin et al. 1991; Kinder and McConaughy 2006; McDermott 1998) to non-Black voters that overcomes the view that Blacks violate cherished American values by appearing intelligent, articulate, hard-working, patriotic, and "clean."[7] These traits help to counter the negative stereotypes often associated with African Americans (Bobo and Kluegel

1997; McDermott 1998) while moving beyond the traditional grassroots advocacy style and issue preferences of prominent Black political figures such as Jesse Jackson and Al Sharpton.

Much of the work on deracialization evaluates the consequences of the strategy based on whether the candidate wins, or his level of support among White voters as a *collective*. We break from this perspective and emphasize that research on deracialization must increase its focus on the individual as the unit of analysis in order to understand the broader dynamics of the strategy. Campaign strategies affect individuals, and the only way to know if they are effective is to study their response. For instance, even when Black candidates attempt to run a deracialized campaign, racialized linkages may always be present (Conover 1984; Mendelberg 2001; Valentino et al. 2002). Candidates typically have little control over how they are presented by the media, political groups, or the public in general (Terkildsen 1993; Terkildsen and Damore 1999; Zilber and Niven 1995). Nor are some Black candidates able to control their phenotypic appearance (e.g., skin color) or their name (e.g., Obama). Thus, we argue that the effectiveness of a deracialization strategy must be evaluated based on the judgments of individuals in the electorate, rather than simply whether the candidate wins.

Racial Consciousness and Political Evaluation

Part of the concern about African American support for Black candidates lies in their viability; but, as we will argue the broader dynamic of support centers on the issue of representing Black interests. We make a clear distinction between group consciousness and simple group identification. Group identification refers to perceived/self-reported membership in a social category (e.g., race, gender, party affiliation) that motivates voters "to favor" one candidate more than others. However, group consciousness is a more politicized view of membership that triggers evaluations of substantive group interests that shape voter preference. Group consciousness has the potential to shape political preferences and behavior aimed at realizing the group's interests. While it is well established that Blacks may use their own race as a political heuristic (Dawson 1994), it is less clear *how* they use candidate race when evaluating Black candidates versus competitive White ones. This is particularly true at the national level.

Group-based identity theories suggests that Blacks would have positive support for, and favor, a Black candidate on the basis of shared racial group membership. A fundamental tenet of identity theory is that discriminatory behavior is related to an individual's degree of identification with the in-group, independent of whether this identification is positive or negative (Oakes et al. 1994; Tajfel and Turner 1986). This is particularly true in low-information settings where individuals are less likely to undertake a rational calculus of the benefits accrued by supporting a particular candidate. Instead voters will use attributes such as race, gender, age, and other descriptive traits to make judgments about candidates. Accordingly, individuals tend to look favorably upon members of their in-group but castigate members of out-groups in order to maintain positive distinctiveness (Brewer 2001). This reasoning suggests that even if African Americans perceive in-group candidates as not representing their interests, they should look upon them more favorably than a candidate of another racial group. This is because one's motivation to have group identity enhanced by the positive evaluations of another in-group member should outweigh substantive policy and political concerns (Brown 1995).

Alternatively, there is substantial evidence to suggest that Black Americans do not naively submit their votes based on candidate race alone. Cross-sectional studies of large numbers of African Americans find high levels (>75 percent) of disagreement that Blacks "should always vote for black candidates when they run" (Walton and Smith 2009). Other research suggests that African Americans exhibit greater levels of political sophistication than one might expect given their, on average, lower levels of education and novice history as an electoral power in national American politics (Glaser 1995). Thus, candidate racial similarity is perhaps only one component of the political decision-making process for African Americans. The others include political information, heuristics related to party identification (Glaser 1995; Tate 1994), and substantive group interests (Tate 2003).

We consider these aforementioned factors and argue against the notion that African Americans will simply give their vote to a Black candidate on the basis of descriptive racial traits alone. Instead, in low-information settings—like the pre-primary stages of the Democratic nomination process—African Americans will use perceived representation of group interests as their political short-cut. It stands that White candidates may also gain positive sentiment from African Americans if they are perceived as either representing Blacks' group interests *or* not being ambivalent to such interests. Thus, one might expect that a candidate like Hillary Clinton would be viewed more favorably by African Americans *if* she is perceived to represent Black interests.

The Case: Hillary Clinton and Barack Obama

Hillary Rodham Clinton has historically enjoyed positive support from African Americans. Among Black respondents in the 1996 American National Election Study (ANES), Bill and Hillary Clinton had the highest feeling thermometer scores out of more than ten political figures with 83.1 and 75.1 points, respectively (Kinder and McConnaughy 2006).[8] These scores outpaced those for Black political figures such as Jesse Jackson, Colin Powell, and Louis Farrakhan. Similarly, the 2000, 2002, and 2004 ANES studies also reported that Bill and Hillary Clinton, respectively, had the highest FT scores among African Americans.

While it is uncertain whether evaluations of Bill and Hillary Clinton are directly related (Burden and Mughan 1999), there is little doubt that as a team the Clintons were extremely popular among African Americans and that the high levels of support during the [Bill] Clinton administration translated into a greater affinity for a Hillary Clinton administration. In fact, in mid to late 2007 Gallup public opinion polls consistently reported that Blacks not only favored Hillary Clinton over Barack Obama by roughly 15–23 percentage points, they were also more likely than Whites to support Hillary Clinton (Newport et al. 2009). Making matters more challenging for Obama, a self-described African American, Clinton received strong public support early on from powerful African American political and social figures.[9]

We speculate that the early Clinton advantage in African American support was heightened by what was presumably Obama's race neutral—deracialization—campaign style.[10] During his campaign, Obama tended to only reference race when describing his own biography, when discussing the historical significance of his candidacy, or when he was forced to confront the issue.[11] He rarely framed his policy positions in reference to racial group concerns and did not advocate for any specific benefits for Blacks. More telling is the fact that early in the race Obama did not promote a large cadre of Black political figures as his surrogates. In his political philosophy in *The Audacity of Hope*, Obama (2006) says quite directly,

> I am a Democrat . . . . and . . . I am a prisoner of my own biography: I can't help but view the American experience through the lens of a Black man of mixed heritage . . . . But that is not all that I am.
>   I reject a politics that is based solely on racial identity, gender identity, sexual orientation, or victimhood generally (10–11).

It would seem that Obama's decision to not overtly, voluntarily, and directly address issues of race likely contributed to the uncertainty among many African Americans who questioned whether he would best represent their interests; and worse, questioned whether he was "black enough" (Ifill 2009). This uncertainty was further intensified by doubts concerning the electability of a Black candidate (Wilson 2008). Finally, because Obama was a newly elected Senator, his own low level of visibility and name recognition further complicated Black voters' perceptions of group interests and the potential for having such interests represented.[12]

To summarize, there are numerous considerations unaccounted for by the existing deracialization research. First, there has not been a high stakes election between viable candidates, one that pits a racial in-group member versus an out-group member, where African Americans are divided on whom to support. Given recent electoral changes, there is reason to believe that such contests will become increasingly frequent. Second, studies of deracialization have not examined perceptions at the individual level. This is largely due to scholars' conception of deracialization as solely an elite-driven campaign strategy. By focusing on perceptions we can learn how individuals respond to candidates who are ostensibly deracialized. Third, studies of deracialization are void of analyses related to perceived race relations. African Americans who perceive race relations as problematic are perhaps more likely to utilize racial group interests as a short-cut; presumably because they desire an elected official who would alleviate the burdens of race. Fourth, studies have yet to examine deracialization at the national level and none have employed a large sample of Black respondents. Without these basic considerations, the research on electoral politics in general and racial politics in specific are left incomplete.

Data

We analyze data collected as part of Gallup's Social Series on Minority Race Relations (MRR). The MRR data contain telephone interviews—conducted June 4–24, 2007—with 2,388 national adults aged eighteen and older. We only analyze data for Whites and African Americans (*n* = 2,098) due to considerations regarding the smaller sample sizes of other racial-ethnic groups interviewed, and because of our targeting questions that primarily speak to White–Black relations. Our final working sample contains 1,032 non-Hispanic Whites, and 796 persons self-described Blacks/African Americans.[13] For results based on this sample, one can say with 95 percent confidence that the maximum margin of sampling error for the working data is ±2.5 percentage points (±3 percent for the White sample, and ±3.5 percent for the Black sample). Importantly, the MRR data contain a diverse cross-section of African Americans, and the employment of such a rich data set supports calls for further public opinion research examining larger samples of African American respondents (Dawson and Cohen 2002; Harris-Lacewell 2007).

Measures and Variables

The 2007 MRR contains a number of measures which inform the questions posed in this paper.[14] For complete information on the measures and their question wording, see the Appendix.

Racial Group Interests. Perceptions of representing Black interests were measured by asking respondents to evaluate which candidate, Hillary Clinton or Barack Obama, would better represent the interests of Blacks in the United States. Aside from the two candidates, respondents could also volunteer "neither," "both," or "unsure."

Candidate Support. Respondents who self-identified as Democrats or leaning Democrats were asked which candidate they were "most likely to support" for the Democratic nomination for president from a list of potential candidates.[15] We mainly analyze a variable comparing the two front-runners in the primary: Obama and Clinton. We also analyze a separate favorability ratings measures for Obama and Clinton. The variables for both candidates were coded favorable (= 1) or unfavorable (= 0).

Racial consciousness—awareness of group concerns including perceived discrimination (Gurin, Hatchett, and Jackson 1989)—was measured by multiple items indicating concerns about race in America. Because scholars often disagree about how to label these components of racial awareness, we define the composite of these items as indicators of *perceived racial context*. We assume thoughts about race and politics are associated with one's political belief system, or schema (Dawson 1994; Kuklinski et al. 1991), and reason that greater awareness or consciousness of racial disparities and unequal treatment—a more negative racial context—would correlate to a greater desire to alleviate the perceived conditions of Black Americans through candidate preference and favorability. If candidates are truly deracialized, we should find that on average perceptions of race play no role in candidate evaluations. Our measure of racial context is based on four sub-concepts: Black–White relations, satisfaction with racial group treatment, perceived racial discrimination, and perceptions of Black–White inequality.

Perceptions of White–Black Relations. Respondents were asked to rate whether race relations between Whites and Blacks are very bad (= 0), somewhat bad (= .33), somewhat good (.66), or very good (= 1) with higher values indicating more positive ratings ($M = .59$, $SD = .23$).

Satisfaction with Racial Group Treatment. Satisfaction with the treatment of Blacks is measured on a scale indicating whether the respondents were very dissatisfied (= 0), somewhat dissatisfied (= .33), somewhat satisfied (= .66), and very satisfied (= 1). Higher values on the scale indicate more satisfaction ($M = .58$, $SD = .31$).

Group Discrimination. Perceptions of discrimination against Blacks are measured with a composite index of five items asking whether respondents believed that Blacks in their community are treated less fairly (= 1) or treated the same or better (= 0) than Whites (1) on the job or at work, (2) in neighborhood shops, (3) retail stores and malls, (4) in a restaurant, bar, theater, or other entertainment place, and (5) in dealings with the police. The summative index of perceived group discrimination is scaled to range from

0 to 1 with higher values indicating greater perceptions of discrimination against Blacks (M = .23, SD = .31).

Racial Inequality. Perceptions of racial inequality are measured with a composite index of three items asking respondents whether Blacks as a group have "as good" (= 0) or lower (= 1) chances as Whites (1) to get jobs for which they are qualified, (2) to get a good education for their children, or (3) to get any housing they can afford. The summative perceived racial inequality index is scaled to range from 0 to 1 with higher values indicating more perceived inequality among Blacks and Whites (M = .24, SD = .33).

The average correlation among the four racial context measures is r = .460 (p < .01), high enough to consider combining the items into a single index. After examining Cronbach alpha (α) measures of internal consistency (i.e., reliability) for both Blacks (α = .669) and Whites (α = .734), a decision was made to use a single composite index of racial context in our multivariate analyses.[16] The index—the average of the four individual measures—ranges from 0 to 1 with higher values indicating a more positive racial context (M = .56, SD = .26).

Demographics.[17] Respondent *race* is constructed from self-reports. Respondents who identified as Black or Black and some other race were coded as "Black." *Sex* is a dummy variable coded 0 for female (55 percent), and 1 for male (45 percent). Age (M = 48, *Median* = 46, SD = 17.2) is measured in years. A four-point ordinal measure of *education*—less than high school (12.5 percent), high school graduate (27 percent), some college (30.5 percent), college graduate (30 percent)—is included, as is a dummy variable indicating whether one has earned a four-year college degree (= 1). Religiosity is measured by frequency of attendance to religious services. Responses were gauged on a five-point ordinal scale of "once a week" (28 percent), "almost every week" (13 percent), "once a month" (13 percent), "seldom" (23 percent), and "never" (22 percent). Household income is an eleven-point ordinal measure (*Median* = $50,000—less than $75,000) ranging from the lowest category of "less than $10,000" to the highest category of "$500,000 or more."

We include three measures related to one's residential living area. *Black Density*—proportion of Blacks living in the statistical metropolitan area of the respondent—is a three category ordinal measure with the values low (= 1), medium (= 2), and high (= 3).[18] *Urbanicity* is also a three category ordinal measure with rural (19 percent), suburban (51 percent), and urban (30 percent) categories. The higher values on this variable are associated with being more urban. *Region* is a categorical variable indicating whether a respondent resides in the South (31 percent), East (23 percent), West (22 percent), or Midwest (24 percent) areas of the United States. This region variable was used to create a dummy variable for *South* (= 1) versus non-South.[19] Black density, urbanicity, and region variables all come from the respondent phone extension file with locations based on the area codes of the sampled households.

Political ideology is measured with a standard five-point scale with response categories of very liberal, liberal, moderate, conservative, and very conservative. The categories were recoded to a three-point ordinal measure combining very liberal and liberal into a single category of liberal (20 percent), very conservative and conservative into a single category of "conservative" (40 percent), and moderate (40 percent) remained a middle category. Accordingly, the variable is coded so that higher values indicate greater liberalism. We are primarily interested in Democratic Party candidates here, so *political party identification* is measured with a single dummy variable indicating whether one is a self-described Democrat or leaning Democrat (49 percent) (= 1), versus an independent (11 percent) or a Republican or leaning Republican (40 percent) (= 0).

We also controlled for race of interviewer to ensure there was no systematic bias related to the interview context (Davis 1997a, 1997b; Krysan and Couper 2003). Forty-two percent of interviews were completed by Black interviewers and 58 percent were completed by non-Black interviewers.[20]

Results

Who Better Represents Black Interests? African Americans were less likely than Whites to believe Obama would better represent Black interests. In fact, African Americans were evenly split between Obama and Clinton on this question. The top section of Table 1 presents these results.

Approximately 45 percent of respondents felt Obama would better represent Blacks' interests, 41 percent believed Clinton would, and 15 percent felt they represented Blacks' interests equally or could not decide between the two. Whites where much more likely to think Obama (56 percent) rather than Clinton (27 percent) represented Black interests, but similar to African Americans, 17 percent either felt the two candidates would equally represent Blacks or could not decide between the two.

Favorability. The middle section of Table 1 shows the favorability ratings across race for two separate items, one for Clinton and another for Obama item. The results indicate that African Americans and Whites each hold generally favorable views toward Clinton and Obama; however, while Whites are more favorable toward Obama (71 percent) than Clinton (54 percent), African Americans hold equal levels of favorability (91 percent each) toward the two candidates.

Candidate Support. Results indicate that in the summer of 2007, most African American Democrats considered only two contenders for the nomination: Clinton and Obama. Together, Clinton (42 percent) and Obama (42 percent) equally split about 84 percent of the African American Democratic preferences.[21] After those two front-runners, only Al Gore (9 percent) and John Edwards (about 5 percent) had support greater than 1 percentage point. The results were much clearer among Whites. White Democrats preferred Clinton (37 percent), over Obama (18 percent), Gore (17 percent), and Edwards (14 percent) by significant margins; and, no other Democratic candidate at that time received greater than 5 percent support.

Unsurprisingly, the results change when Republican candidates, and self-identifying Republican respondents, are considered; especially, along racial lines. The bottom section of Table 1 shows the breakdown of Republican *and* Democrat candidate preferences across race. Now, both Clinton's (19 percent) and Obama's (9 percent) support are cut in half among Whites, but among African Americans both equally drop only 4 percentage points.

Paired with the finding regarding favorability and beliefs about who would better represent Black interests, the data show Clinton and Obama were initially the strongest contenders for African Americans' votes.[22] The lack of a clear majority for either Obama or Clinton on the matter of Black group interests provides empirical support for the claim that Obama was *somewhat* deracialized but *primarily among African Americans*.

Table 1.
Racial Differences in Candidate Preferences, Favorability Ratings, and Perceived Representation of Black Interests

Candidate Represents Black Interests[a]	Whites	Blacks
Clinton represents Black interests better	27%	41%
	(342)	(319)
Obama represents interests better	56%	45%
	(717)	(349)
No clear choice (DK or both)	17%	15%
	(219)	(115)
Totals	100%	100%
	(1278)	(783)
Candidate Favorability	**Whites**	**Blacks**
Obama favorability[b]	71%	91%
	(994)	(646)
Clinton favorability[c]	54%	91%
	(1242)	(754)
Candidate Preference[d]	**Whites**	**Blacks**
Barack Obama	9%	38%
	(125)	(244)
Hillary Clinton	19%	38%
	(248)	(253)
Other Democrat	22%	14%
	(232)	(105)
Republican	49%	10%
	(442)	(52)
Total	100%	100%
	(1047)	(654)

Notes: [a]χ^2 ($df = 2$) = 43.9, $p < .01$; [b]$t(df = 1636.1)$ = 10.9, $p < .01$; [c]$t(df = 1984)$ = 21.4, $p < .01$; [d]χ^2 ($df = 3$) = 320.5, $p < .01$.

Whites perceived Obama as more likely than Clinton to represent Black interests suggesting he might be easily racialized as the election went forward.

Perceived Racial Context and Black Interests

The extent to which a candidate is deracialized might also depend on one's [racial] beliefs (Kuklinski et al. 1991); whether individuals perceive a connection between their judgments about who will represent racial interests and perceptions that racial interests need to be met and ostensibly dealt with. If a candidate is more racialized then perceptions related to the context of race relations—whether they are more positive or negative—should be highly correlated with a belief that the political figure will better represent Black interests; but, if perceptions of the candidate's group related interests are weakly tied to racial context then the candidate is ostensibly deracialized. In essence, deracialization is the absence of a connection between a candidate and racial considerations.

Our measures of association reveal a significant but weak relationship ($\eta = .069$, $p < .05$) between racial context and perceptions of whether Obama or Clinton, or both equally, represent Black interests, but after controlling for racial group identification the relationship was non-significant for both groups (African Americans: $\eta = .086$, *n.s.*; Whites: $\eta = .071$, *n.s.*). Thus, views on Black–White race relations appear to be independent of views on who would better represent the interests of Blacks; at least among self-identified Democrats who were asked the question. These results are shown in Table 2. The findings further suggest that Africans Americans perceived Obama (and perhaps Clinton) to be deracialized. Moreover, although Whites perceived Obama would better represent Black interests, they did not strongly connect these perceptions with their views on race relations.

Narrowing the Analysis: African American Public Opinion

There are few contemporary studies examining African American public opinion at the inception of the first African American president's election. Thus, this analysis is a relatively unique attempt to study empirically what happens early in the campaign process as African American candidates navigate issues of racial identity and public perceptions. The remainder of our findings center on African American respondents.

Having established that (1) there were two main challengers, one White and one Black, for the votes of African Americans, (2) both were viewed equally favorably

Table 2.
Perceived Representation of Black Interests and Racial Context Measures

		Perceptions of Racial Context		
	Who Better Represents Black Interests	M	SD	N
Whites	Clinton	.64	.23	289
	Obama	.66	.23	593
	No clear choice	.69	.25	143
	Total	.66	.23	1025
	$F(2,1022) = 2.58$, *n.s.*, $\eta = .071$			
Blacks	Clinton	.44	.23	278
	Obama	.39	.23	311
	No clear choice	.41	.25	77
	Total	.41	.23	666
	$F(2,663) = 2.47$, *n.s.*, $\eta = .086$			

Notes: Perceptions of Racial Context Scores range from 0 to 1 with higher scores indicating more positive context (i.e., low discrimination and racial conflict).

among African Americans, (3) both were viewed equally in terms of their representation of Black interests, and (4) perceptions of who better represented Black interests were not correlated with perceptions about the climate and context of Black–White relations, we now turn our analysis to a specific question of why Obama did not overwhelmingly receive African American's support. Did African Americans penalize Obama because it was not clear he represented their group interests?

As we have argued, African Americans may hold Obama to a higher standard because of who he is: African American. Obama clearly considers himself African American, and has not shied away from his racial background, but he also presented a different image of the stereotypical Black political figure. Additionally, around the period when the MRR study was conducted, African American leaders such as Jesse Jackson openly questioned Obama's authenticity and many African American voters appear to have had similar concerns (Ifill 2009).

The data reveal that among those African Americans who believe Hillary Clinton will better represent Black interest, 22 percent have an unfavorable view of Obama. This is compared to the 11 percent of those who believe Obama will better represent Black interests and have an unfavorable view of Hillary Clinton. When there is no clear choice regarding who will better represent Black interests, unfavorable views are equal for Obama and Clinton. These results indicate supporters of Hillary Clinton by way of representation of Black interests have a more negative view of Barack Obama, than Obama supporters have of Clinton. Moreover, lower favorability toward Obama and Clinton significantly affect expressed support for the two.

Among those African American Democrats who hold unfavorable views of Obama, a majority of them choose to support Clinton (64 percent) or some other Democratic candidate (36 percent). Yet, among those who hold unfavorable views of Clinton, there is no clear majority; half support Obama (50 percent) and half support some other Democratic candidate (50 percent). While not conclusive, these data certainly suggests some African Americans held misgivings about Barack Obama in-part because he was not perceived as acting in their best group interests.

How rigorous are these findings? To find out, we ran logistic regression analyses to predict favorable (1) [versus unfavorable (0)] evaluations of Obama and Clinton separately.

The regression analyses produced coefficients (B) and their standard errors (SE) indicating strength and direction of any effects, and significance tests are provided to assist in ruling out the probability the estimates occur due to chance. The analyses also produce adjusted odds ratios (*Exp(B)* in the table, and "*OR*" henceforth) which indicate the change in odds of a favorable response given a one unit increase the predictor or independent variables. ORs greater than one indicates a positive effect and ORs less than one indicate a negative effect. The Nagelkerke *R2* statistic represents an overall measure indicating the predictive ability of the model; it represents the proportion of variance in favorability evaluations due to the set of variables in the regression analyses. The log-likelihood statistic (*−2LL*) is an additional measure of model fit based on a Chi-Square test with k degrees of freedom (k = number of newly estimated coefficients), and it indicates whether additional variables in a model have a significant effect.[23] The *−2LL* statistic operates off a "lower is better" criterion.

Table 3.
Logistic Regression Predicting Favorable Views of Obama and Clinton (African American Respondents)

	Favorability Toward Obama (n = 558)						Favorability Toward Clinton (n = 611)					
	B	SE	Exp(B)	B	SE	Exp(B)	B	SE	Exp(B)	B	SE	Exp(B)
Constant	-1.73	1.36	.18	-.80	1.43	.45	.76	1.16	2.14	.62	1.18	.82
Sex (male = 1)	.04	.34	1.04	-.04	.37	.96	-.98**	.33	.38	-.94**	.33	.39
Education level	.38*	.18	1.47	.38*	.19	1.46	.19	.18	1.21	.21	.18	1.23
Age	.01	.01	1.01	.01	.01	1.01	-.01	.01	.99	-.01	.01	.99
Region (South = 1)	-.38	.33	.68	-.39	.35	.67	.02	.33	1.02	-.01	.33	.99
Income level	.17	.10	1.19	.12	.10	1.12	-.08	.09	.92	-.08	.09	.92
Residential Black density	-.21	.31	.81	-.33	.34	.72	.20	.24	1.23	.21	.24	1.23
Political ideology (liberalism)	.47*	.23	1.60	.33	.24	1.39	-.21	.22	.81	-.18	.22	.84
Party identification (Dem = 1)	1.81**	.35	6.12	1.97**	.39	7.16	2.01**	.35	7.44	2.03**	.35	7.59
Religious attendance	.04	.12	1.04	.01	.13	1.01	.31**	.11	1.37	.33**	.12	1.39
Race of interviewer (Black = 1)	-.30	.33	.74	-.22	.35	.81	.09	.33	1.09	.06	.33	1.06
Racial context	.33	.71	1.39	.62	.76	1.85	-.09	.67	.92	-.10	.67	.91
Obama better represents Black interests over Clinton				1.11**	.22	3.04				-.19	.17	.82
Model Fit												
Nagelkerke R²	.22			.33			.21			.21		
-2LL	275.08**			242.65**			293.32**			292.06		

*Notes: *p < .05; **p < .01*

Favorability. The results—shown in Table 3—indicate that African Americans' beliefs about who will better represent their interests are a key predictor of favorability towards Obama, but not Clinton. The odds of having a favorable view of Obama increase significantly if one believes he will better represent Black interests; yet beliefs about Clinton being a better representative of Black interests have no significant effect on her favorability. Even after controlling for a number of factors, including party identification and perceived racial context, African Americans tend to have more positive views of Hillary Clinton regardless of whether or not they believe she will be a better representative of Black interests; yet, they tend to hold Obama to a different standard.

Ideology and gender are also noteworthy factors in the analysis. The more liberal one is, the more likely he or she is to have a favorable view of Obama. The only significant predictor of favorable views of Clinton is sex: African American males have a less favorable view of Hillary Clinton than African American women. Ancillary analysis (not presented in a table) shows that controlling for the same variables in Table 3, African American Democratic women are significantly more likely than men to support Hillary Clinton as their first choice ($B = -1.02$, $p < .05$, $OR = .36$). However, one's sex has no significant effect on support for Obama. This is a significant finding and one that was alluded to in popular national discourse around what American needs first, a woman president or a Black president.

Candidate Support. Attitudes toward candidates are one thing, but expressed candidate preference is another. We also ran a logistic regression analysis predicting whether perceptions of substantive representation might also predict candidate support (1 = Obama, 0 = Clinton). These results are shown in Table 4. With the same variables, plus the favorability ratings, from the previous analysis included as controls, we found that not only did perceptions of racial group interest predict support for Obama over Clinton, but they mediated the impact of positive views of Clinton.

When our measure of Black interests representation was not included in the model, Africans Americans who had a favorable view of Hillary Clinton were significantly less likely to support Obama over Clinton ($B = -2.43$, $SE = 1.08$, $p < .05$, $OR = .09$). However, when we include those interests perceptions, not only does it dominate the model ($B = 1.29$, $SE = .13$, $p < .01$, $OR = 3.64$, $\Delta R^2 = .27$, $p < .01$), but now having a favorable view of Clinton has no effect ($B = 1.96$, $SE = 1.24$, *n.s.*, $OR = .14$) on support for Obama over Clinton. Clearly, when it came to favorability ratings, and expressed support for Obama during the early part of his candidacy, questions about substantive representation occupied much of the thinking of the African American electorate.

Discussion and Conclusions

We find that among African Americans, perceptions of racial group interests are a stronger predictor of both favorability and support for Obama. While his White female rival, Hillary Clinton, was just as likely to be perceived as being able to represent Black interests, these perceptions had no statistically significant effect on her favorability ratings. In our last analysis we found that favorable views of Hillary Clinton yielded lower support for Obama; however, when perceptions of group interests were included in the model, Clinton's favorability advantage disappeared.

Table 4.
Logistic Regression Predicting Candidate Support for Obama
(African American Respondents)

	Candidate Support for Obama (1) versus Clinton (0) (n = 416)					
	B	*SE*	*Exp(B)*	*B*	*SE*	*Exp(B)*
Constant	1.10	1.34	3.00	1.24	1.54	3.46
Sex (male = 1)	.52*	.23	1.69	.42	.27	1.53
Education level	.30*	.12	1.35	.22	.14	1.24
Age	−.01	.01	.99	−.01	.01	.99
Region (South = 1)	−.08	.22	.92	−.07	.25	.94
Income level	.10	.06	1.10	.08	.07	1.08
Residential Black density	−.16	.19	.85	−.20	.21	.82
Political ideology (liberalism)	.52**	.15	1.68	.45**	.17	1.56
Religious attendance	.04	.08	1.04	−.01	.10	.99
Race of interviewer (Black = 1)	−.31	.22	.74	−.23	.25	.79
Racial context	−.73	.51	.48	−.50	.60	.61
Clinton favorability rating	−2.43*	1.08	.09	−1.96	1.24	.14
Obama better represents Black interests over Clinton				1.29**	.13	3.64
			Model Fit			
Nagelkerke R^2	.18			.45		
-2LL	514.78**			402.86**		
N	416			416		

Notes: *p < .05; **p < .01

We also find that measures of perceived racial context mattered very little in the early parts of the 2007 election season. While African Americans perceived a more negative racial context than Whites, these beliefs were not significantly related to candidate support, favorability ratings of Democratic candidates Clinton and Obama, or perceptions of which candidate is better able to represent Blacks' interests. The lack of an association between racial thinking and candidate evaluations provides more evidence, albeit less direct, that Obama (and Clinton) was more or less viewed as deracialized.

On a related matter, we did find that African American females were more likely to have a favorable view of Clinton than African American males. The implication is that perhaps gender was also connected to differential views toward the candidates. The sex difference finding also suggests that racial identity is fluid, and that the strength of racial group perceptions vary across issues, spaces, and allegiances. A future study might include an analysis of "Women's interests," similar to our consideration of racial interests herein.

Taken as a whole, our findings indicate that Blacks may undertake a more sophisticated decision-making calculus than the often assumed same-race heuristic, particularly when they are evaluating an ostensibly deracialized candidate, one who is perceived as less likely than another candidate to better represent Blacks' interests. Therefore, while much of the literature on Black candidate behavior centers on the benefits of attaining White support, there is much more to be said about how these perceptions affect Black support. To the point, deracialized electoral strategies are relevant to both Black candidates and Black voters.

For much of American history, African Americans' life chances have been defined by race. In turn, race became an effective decision-making heuristic for individual Blacks, shaping their political thinking and preferences. Over time, Blacks' political fate has evolved to closely mirror that of most other Americans. This change in political context has provided increased space for Black candidates to develop their own political identities, but it has also increased the challenges for winning higher offices and the subsequent opportunities for non-Black candidates to effectively court Black voters.

Deracialization attempts typically occur at the campaign level but from the standpoint of political behavior they matter most at the individual level. In order for a candidate to be considered deracialized, members of the electorate must actually disconnect their beliefs about race to the candidate when the two are considered in the same vein.

Rather than viewing a candidate as wholly racial or wholly non-racial, voters judge candidates relative to others based on their likelihood of being sensitive to or supportive of issues or racial group concern. Though group identity theories suggests that individuals are more likely to perceive fellow group members more positively than outgroup members (Kramer and Brewer 1984; Tajfel and Turner 1985), we have argued that shared racial group membership is not sufficient for garnering Black voters' support. Instead, questions of substantive representation tend to influence African Americans' support levels while also setting different expectation standards unique to Black candidates.

Black candidates for statewide and national office such as Artur Davis, Deval Patrick, Harold Ford, Alan Keyes, Ken Blackwell, and Lynn Swann all operate in an era where a strict reliance on racial group appeals is viewed by many Whites, and a small percentage of Black, as less desirable and less effective. It is within this era that Barack Obama emerged as the most viable Black candidate to ever seek the highest office in the land. Forty years after Shirley Chisholm became the first African American to run for President, Obama's candidacy highlights the complex and often tenuous relationship between group identity and politics in the United States.

Our research directs attention to the need to continuously revisit older concepts in the racial politics literature to assess their conceptual and empirical viability in the wake of racial progress. Yet, to some degree our results and conclusions are incomplete; our findings raise many more questions than answers. Will Obama become the baseline judgment for Black political candidates, or is he considered atypical? Is deracialization fluid or fixed; can individuals be deracialized one moment, then racialized the next? How does one measure the success or failure of a deracialization strategy? All of these questions are interesting, but not answerable with our data or analysis. Public opinion surveys are key to understanding these issues, but many studies are marred by poor measures of relevant concepts, and relatively small samples of African Americans. Thus, the key to progressing the understanding of Black political behavior will lie in the ability of researchers to gain access to quality individual level data during all phases of a campaign.

As for the future of Black political candidates, our findings suggest there will be challenges ahead. They must address concerns about racial issues while avoiding the appearance of being "too liberal." Artur Davis, a Democratic congressman from Alabama, lost his 2010 Democratic primary to Alabama's Agriculture commission, Ron Sparks. Davis was a lifelong Democrat, had legislative experience, was Harvard educated, and chaired Obama's campaign in the state. Yet, analysts say he lost his election because he did not vote for a controversial Democratic health care bill—an attempt to be less liberal—and openly rejected support from African American political organizations. African American constituents penalized Davis by supporting his White opponent (Sparks) who won the primary by about 28 percent points. If, in fact, deracialization strategies erode support among African American voters, Black candidates will likely have to spend more time on narrow segments of the electorate later in the campaign. Moving forward, scholars should keep a keen eye on how both Black and White (and other candidates) navigate issues related to race, as well as the extent to which candidates are seen through a racial lens in the broader public.

Appendix: Study Variables

Favorability Ratings of Clinton and Obama

Q30. Next, we'd like to get your overall opinion of some people in the news. As I read each name, please say if you have a favorable (= 1) or unfavorable (= 0) opinion of these people. How about (read candidate)?

A. Hillary Clinton

F. Barack Obama

Representation of Black Interests

Q36. In your view, which candidate would do the better job of representing the interests of Blacks in the United States? Hillary Clinton (=–1), Barack Obama (= 1), or Same/No Difference (= 0)?

Choice for Nominee

Q33. (Asked only Democrats and Leaning Democrats): Next, I'm going to read a list of people who may be running in the Democratic primaries for president in the next election. After I read all the names, please tell me which of those candidates you would be most likely to support for the Democratic nomination for President in the year 2008, or if you would support someone else.

Perceptions o f Racial Inequality

Q8. In general, do you think that Blacks have as good a chance as Whites in your community to get any kind of job for which they are qualified (= 0), or don't you think they have as good a chance (= 1)?

Q9. In general, do you think that Black children have as good a chance as White children in your community to get a good education (= 0), or don't you think they have as good a chance (= 1)?

Q10. Again, in general, do you think that Blacks have as good a chance as Whites in your community to get any housing they can afford (= 0), or don't you think they have as good a chance (= 1)?

Perceived Group Discrimination

Q11. Just your impression, are Blacks in your community treated less fairly than Whites in the following situations? How about (read statement)? (Yes, treated LESS fairly = 1, No, treated same/better = 0)

A. On the job or at work

B. In neighborhood shops

C. In stores downtown or in the shopping mall

D. In restaurants, bars, theaters, or other entertainment places

E. In dealing with the police, such as traffic incidents

Perceived Personal Discrimination

Q12. [Only asked of Black respondents] Can you think of any occasion in the last thirty days when you felt you were treated unfairly in the following places because you were Black? How about (read statement)? (Yes, treated LESS fairly = 1, No, treated same/better = 0)

A. At your place of work

B. In a store where you were shopping

D. In a restaurant, bar, theater, or other entertainment place

E. In dealings with the police, such as traffic incidents

Satisfaction with Racial Group Treatment

Q5C. We'd like to know how you feel about the way various groups in society are treated. For each of the following groups, please say whether you are very satisfied (= 4), somewhat satisfied (= 3), somewhat dissatisfied (= 2), or very dissatisfied (= 1) with the way they are treated. How about Blacks?

Perceptions of White–Black Relations

Q6A. We'd like to know how you would rate relations between various groups in the United States these days. Would you say relations between Whites and Blacks are very good (= 4), somewhat good (= 3), somewhat bad (= 2), or very bad (= 1)?

Demographics

Partisanship (D9, D9A): In politics, as of today, do you consider yourself a Republican, a Democrat, or an Independent? As of today, do you lean more to the Democratic Party or the Republican Party?

Household Income

The complete codes for household income are as follows: 1 = Less than $10K, 2 = $10–$20K, 3 = $20–$30K, 4 = $30–$40K, 5 = $40K–$50K, 6 = $50–$75K, 7 = $75K–$99k, 8 = $100K–$149K, 9 = $150k–$249K, 10 = $250k–$499K, and 11 = $500K and over.

Political Ideology: D10. How would you describe your political views (very conservative – 1, conservative (= 2), moderate (= 3), liberal (= 4), or very liberal (= 5)

Sex (QD1/S2): Interviewer recorded

Age (QD2): Please tell me your age.

Education: QD3. What is the last grade or class that you completed in school?

Religiosity: QD24. How often do you attend church or synagogue? At least once a week (= 5), almost every week (= 4), about once a month (= 3), seldom (= 2), or never (= 1)?

Notes

1. Alan Keyes' Senate run in Illinois, Lynn Swann's Gubertorial bid in Pennsylvania, Willie Herenton in Tennessee, and Al Sharpton and Carolyn Mosely-Braun's bids for the Democratic Presidential nomination are a few classic instances. And, a more recent example is Artur Davis' failed Gubernatorial Democratic primary campaign in Alabama, where African Americans largely supported Ron Sparks, a White candidate.

2. Much of this critique, however, rests at the point of conjecture. For example, recent media and anecdotal accounts cite Barack Obama's historic election as the United States' first African American President as the ultimate culmination of a successful race neutral electoral strategy.

3. In a larger field of pre-primary candidates, policy issues via priorities may matter (Aldrich and Alvarez 1994), but differentiation is more difficult. Voters are operating in a low-information setting that increases the likelihood that they will rely on more descriptive factors as decision-making heuristics. Thus, the early stages of the presidential campaign provide an ideal time frame for understanding voter evaluations and expectations.

4. We consider Obama to be "Black" (or African American) because he himself undertakes this identification (Obama 2006). By doing so, we do not ignore the commentary regarding whether some African Americans (and White Americans) question whether Obama is "Black enough."

5. It is important to clarify at the outset that we use the Obama–Clinton contest as emblematic of broader racialized candidate evaluations. As we will show, early on the candidates were liked and perceived at equal levels among African Americans; thus, it provides a good example of the actions candidates must adopt early on to shore up support early or risk losing.

6. Deracialization does not mean that candidates are silent on race, it simply means that racialization is not a prominent component of their winning strategy.

7. Consider, for example, the controversial remarks of Senate Majority Leader Harry Reid (D-NV) who in 2008 described Obama's appeal as a "clean, light-skinned [Black]" who speaks with no "Negro dialect." Vice President Joe Biden made similar comments in describing his then opponent for the Democratic nomination (Heilemann and Halpern 2010, 37).

8. The ANES measures affect toward political figures through feeling thermometer (FT) ratings. The ratings range from "0" (indicating the least warm) to "100" (indicating the warmest feelings).

9. Some of the early endorsers of Hillary Clinton include NBA Hall of Famer Earvin "Magic" Johnson, entertainer 50 cent, Entrepreneur Robert L. Johnson, Legal Executive and former President Clinton advisor Vernon Jordan, and Congress members Charlie Rangel (D-NY), John Lewis (D-GA), Sheila Jackson-Lee (D-TX), and the late Stephanie Tubbs-Jones (D-OH).

10. An important question that is beyond the scope of this paper is how one disentangles candidates' normative beliefs about what "should" be done in terms of policy (i.e., their principles), versus the strategy they use to get elected (e.g., their politics). The extant literature on deracialization strategies may suggest that Black political figures are trying to covertly win elections by not promoting issues they really want to promote. That is, the strategy is an intentional avoidance of race, rather than the likelihood that a candidate genuinely believes that one should avoid racial issues in general. J.C. Watts, Alan Keyes, and Obama, all represent examples of this confounding political orientation milieu.

11. Most notably, Obama's Philadelphia speech on race was delivered in reaction to the controversy over remarks made by his former Pastor, Reverend Jeremiah Wright. We view the speech, and the pressure to confront issues of race as reminiscent of John F. Kennedy's Speech on Religion where he acknowledged his Catholic identity but emphasized that, "there are real issues which should decide this campaign. And they are not religious issues . . . for war and hunger and ignorance and despair know no religious barriers." Whenever race rears its head, Obama offers the same characterization of the issues the country faces.

12. In a December 2006 Gallup Poll, 47 percent of respondents did not offer an opinion about whether they had a favorable or unfavorable view of Obama. A little over six months later, a July 2007, Gallup Poll found that that Obama still had name recognition problems. He received a relatively high number of "never heard of" responses when asked their favorability ratings for potential Democratic party nominees, including 14 percent from the overall sample, 7 percent of Whites, 14 percent of Blacks, and 43 percent of Hispanics.

13. The final data are weighted using the normalized adjusted weights provided by Gallup.

14. All volunteered responses, including "don't know," "unsure," and refusals responses were coded as missing, and excluded from the analyses.

15. The list included Delaware Senator, Joe Biden; New York Senator, Hillary Clinton; Connecticut Senator, Christopher Dodd; former North Carolina Senator, John Edwards; former Vice President, Al Gore;

former Alaska Senator, Mike Gravel; Ohio Congressman, Dennis Kucinich; Illinois Senator, Barack Obama; and New Mexico Governor, Bill Richardson.

16. We used the term "index" instead of scale because with the former, the levels of the composite indicate the amount of the concept being measure, whereas with the latter, the levels of the composite depend on the underlying construct. We assume that each sub-indicator of the index contributes equally to the overall level of racial context.

17. The descriptive demographic data below are weighted (sample weight by region and race) to reflect their representative proportions in the larger population of U.S. adults, age eighteen and older.

18. Because we were not able to identify the specific geographic basis for the Black population estimates (e.g., congressional district, zip code, statistical metropolitan area), we used the Black density variable as an indicator of racial context. The Black density variable is used to create the sampling parameters for the oversampling of Black respondents. The Black density variable has a .643 association with the actual "percent black" information found in the MRR dataset.

19. The Southern region includes Virginia, North Carolina, South Carolina, Georgia, Florida, Kentucky, Tennessee, Alabama, Mississippi, Arkansas, Louisiana, Oklahoma, and Texas; East region includes Maine, New Hampshire, Vermont, Massachusetts, Rhode Island, New York, New Jersey, Pennsylvania, Maryland, Delaware, West Virginia, and District of Columbia; Midwest region includes Ohio, Michigan, Indiana, Illinois, Wisconsin, Minnesota, Iowa, Missouri, South Dakota, Nebraska, and Kansas; and the West region includes Montana, Arizona, Colorado, Idaho, Utah, Nevada, New Mexico, California, Oregon, Washington, and Hawaii.

20. White interviewers comprise most of the non-Black interviewer category. Of the total interviews completed by non-Black interviewers, 90 percent of them were completed by White interviewers, followed by Hispanic interviewers with 8 percent, and Asian/Pacific Islander interviewers with 2 percent.

21. This analysis using the MRR data is mainly focused on Democrats, Clinton and Obama, yet self-identified African American Republicans also had their preferences. Responses from the MRR study show that among Republican candidates (Kansas Senator Sam Brownback, former Virginia Governor Jim Gilmore, former Speaker of the House Newt Gingrich, former New York City Mayor Rudy Giuliani, Nebraska Senator Chuck Hagel, former Arkansas Governor Mike Huckabee, California Congressman Duncan Hunter, Arizona Senator John McCain, former Massachusetts Governor Mitt Romney, Colorado Congressman Tom Tancredo, former Wisconsin Governor Tommy Thompson, former Tennessee Senator, Fred Thompson, and Texas Congressman Ron Paul), 31 percent of African Americans said "none" of the candidates listed were their first choice, 27 percent said Rudy Giuliani was their first choice, 11 percent said John McCain was their first choice, and the remaining percentages were spread across the other candidates.

22. Contrary to previous research, we find no evidence of race of interviewer effects on our main variables. Statistically, Black and non-Black interviewers received similar responses for favorability evaluations of Obama ($\chi^2 = 3.01$, $df = 1$, $p = .08$) and Clinton ($\chi^2 = .55$, $df = 1$, $p = .46$), perceptions about who better serves Blacks' interests ($\chi^2 = 2.90$, $df = 2$, $p = .23$), and choice for president between Clinton and Obama ($\chi^2 = 3.01$, $df = 1$, $p = .08$).

23. The $-2LL$ for Model 1 shows the improvement from a baseline of no predictors, and the $-2LL$ for Model 2 indicates whether any additional variables significantly improve the model's statistical fit.

References

Aldrich, John H. and Michael R. Alvarez. 1994. "Issues and the Presidential Primary Voter." *Political Behavior* 16: 289–318.

Bobo, Larry D. 1988. "Attitudes toward the Black Political Movement: Trends, Meaning, and Effects of Racial Policy Preferences." *Social Psychology Quarterly* 51. 287–302.

Bobo, Lawrence and James Kluegel. 1997. "Status, Ideology, and Dimensions of Whites' Racial Beliefs and Attitudes: Progress and Stagnation." In *Racial Attitudes in the 1990s: Continuity and Change*, edited by Stephen Tuch and Jack Martin, 93–120. Westport, CT: Praeger.

Brewer, Marylin B. 2001. "Ingroup Identification and Intergroup Conflict." In *Social Identity, Intergroup Conflict and Conflict Resolution*, edited by Richard D. Ashmore, Lee J. Jussim, and David Wilder. Oxford: Oxford University Press.

Brown, Ruppert. 1995. *Prejudice: It's Social Psychology*. Oxford: Blackwell Press.

Burden, Barry C. and Anthony Mughan. 1999. "Public Opinion and Hillary Rodham Clinton." *Public Opinion Quarterly* 63: 237–50.

Citrin, Jack, Donald Philip Green, and David O. Sears. 1990. "White Reactions to Black Candidates: When Does Race Matter?" *Public Opinion Quarterly* 54: 74–96.

Collet, Christian. 2008. "Minority Candidates, Alternative Media, and Multiethnic America: Deracializaiton or Toggling? *Perspectives on Politics* 6: 707–28.

Conover, Pamela. 1984. "The Influence of Group Identifications on Political Perception and Evaluation." *Journal of Politics* 46: 760–85

Cox, Gary W. and Matthew D. McCubbins. 1991. "On the Decline of Party Voting in Congress." *Legislative Studies Quarterly* 16: 547–70.

Davis, Darren W. 1997a. "The Direction of Race of Interviewer Effects among African-Americans: Donning the Black Mask." *American Journal of Political Science* 41: 309–22.

———. 1997b. "Nonrandom Measurement Error and Race of the Interviewer Effects among African Americans." *Public Opinion Quarterly* 61: 183–207.

Dawson, Michael C. 1994. *Behind the Mule: Race and Class in African-American Politics*. Princeton, NJ: Princeton University Press.

Dawson, Michael C. and Cathy J. Cohen. 2002. "Problems in the Study of the Politics of Race." In *Political Science State of the Discipline*, edited by Ira Katnelson and Helen Milner. Washington, DC: W.W. Norton.

Gillespie, Andra. 2009. *Whose Black Politics? Cases in Post-Racial Black Leadership*. New York: Routledge.

Glaser, James M. 1995. "Black and White Perceptions of Party Differences." *Political Behavior* 17: 155–77.

Goffman, Erving. 1959. *The Presentation of Self in Everyday Life*. New York: Doubleday Anchor.

Gurin, Patricia, Shirley Hatchett, and James S. Jackson. 1989. *Hope and Independence: Blacks' Response to Electoral and Party Politics*. New York: Russell Sage.

Hajnal. Zoltan L. 2006. *Changing White Attitudes toward Black Political Leadership*. Cambridge: Cambridge University Press.

Hamilton, Charles V. 1977. "Deracialization: Examination of a Political Strategy," *First World* 1: 3–5.

Harris-Lacewell, Melissa V. 2007. "Political Science and the Study of African American Public Opinion." In *African American Perspectives on Political Science*, edited by Wilber C. Rich. Philadelphia, PA: Temple University Press.

Heilemann, John and Mark Halperin 2010. *Game Change: Obama and the Clintons, McCain and Palin, and the Race of a Lifetime*. New York: HarperCollins.

Ifill, Gwen. 2009. *The Breakthrough: Politics and Race in the Age of Obama*. New York: Random House.

Jones, Charles E., and Michael L. Clemons. 1993. "A Model of Racial Crossover." In *Dilemmas of Black Politics*, edited by Georgia Persons, 66–84. New York: Harper Collins College Publishers.

Kinder, Donald R. and Corrine M. McConnaughy. 2006. "Military Triumph, Racial Transcendence, and Colin Powell," *Public Opinion Quarterly* 70: 139–65.

Kramer, Roderick M. and Marilynn B. Brewer. 1984. "Effects of Group Identity on Resource Use in a Simulated Commons Dilemma." *Journal of Personality and Social Psychology* 46: 1044–57.

Kuklinski, James H., Robert C. Luskin, and John Bolland. 1991. "Where Is the Schema? Going Beyond the 'S' Word in Political Psychology." *American Political Science Review* 85: 1341–56.

Kuklinski, James H. and Paul J. Quirk. 2000. "Reconsidering the Rational Public: Cognition, Heuristics, and Mass Opinion." In *Elements of Reason: Cognition, Choice, and the Bounds of Rationality*, edited by Arthur Lupia, Matthew D. McCubbins, and Samuel L. Popkin, 153–82. Cambridge: Cambridge University Press.

Krysan, Maria and Mick P. Couper. 2003. "Race in the Live and the Virtual Interview: Racial Deference, Social Desirability, and Activation Effects in Attitude Surveys." *Social Psychology Quarterly* 66: 364–83.

Lau, Richard. 1989. "Individual and Contextual Influences on Group Identification." *Social Psychology Quarterly* 52 (September): 220–31.

Lui, Baodong. 2003. "Deracialization and Urban Racial Contexts." *Urban Affairs Review* 38: 572–91.

Mansbridge, Jane. 1999. "Should Blacks Represent Blacks and Women Represent Women? A Contingent 'Yes.'" *Journal of Politics* 61: 628–57.

McCormick, Joseph P., II and Charles E. Jones. 1993. "The Conceptualization of Deracialization." In *Dilemmas of Black Politics*, edited by Georgia Persons. New York: Harper Collins College Publishers.

McGraw, Kathleen M. 2002. "Manipulating Public Opinion." In *Understanding Public Opinion*, edited by Barbara Norrander and Clyde Wilcox., 2nd edn. Washington, DC: CQ Press.

McDermott, Monika. 1998. "Race and Gender Cues in Low-Information Elections." *Political Research Quarterly* 51: 895–918.

Mendelberg, Tali. 2001. *The Race Card: Campaign Strategy, Implicit Messages, and the Norm of Equality*. Princeton, NJ: Princeton University Press.

Neuman, W. Russell, George E. Marcus, Ann M. Crigler, and Michael Mackuen. 2007. *The Affect Effect: Dynamics of Emotion in Political Thinking and Behavior*. Chicago, IL: University of Chicago Press.

Newport, Frank, Jeffrey M. Jones, Lydia Saad, Alec M. Gallup, and Fred L. Israel. 2009. *Winning the White House 2008: The Gallup Poll, Public Opinion, and the Presidency*. New York: Checkmark Books.

Oakes, Penelope J., S. Alex Haslam, and John C. Turner. 1994. *Stereotyping and Social Reality*. Oxford, and Cambridge, MA: Blackwell.

Obama, Barack H. 2006. *The Audacity of Hope: Thoughts on Reclaiming the American Dream*. New York: Crown Publishers.

Orey, Byron D'Andra. 2006. "Deracialization or Racialization: The Making of a Black Mayor in Jackson, Mississippi." *Politics and Policy* 34: 814–36.

Peffley, Mark and Jon Hurwitz. 1998. "Whites' Stereotypes of Blacks: Sources and Political Consequences," In *Perception and Prejudice: Race and Politics in the United States*, edited by Jon Hurwitz and Mark Peffley. New Haven, CT: Yale University Press.

Perry, Huey L. 1996. *Race, Politics and Governance in the United States*. Gainesville, FL: University Press of Florida.

Pohlman, Marcus and Michael Kirby. 1996. *Racial Politics at the Crossroads*. Knoxville, TN: University of Tennessee Press.

Popkin, Samuel L. 1991. *The Reasoning Voter: Communication and Persuasion in Presidential Campaigns*. Chicago, IL: University of Chicago Press.

Reese, Laura and Ronald E. Brown. 1995. "Full Access the Effects of Religious Messages on Racial Identity and System Blame among African Americans." *Journal of Politics* 57: 24–43.

Reeves, Keith. 1997. *Voting Hopes or Fears? White Voters, Black Candidates, and Racial Politics in America*. Oxford: Oxford University Press.

Tajfel, Henri and John C. Turner. 1986. "The Social Identity Theory of Inter-group Behavior." In *Psychology of Intergroup Relations*, edited by William G. Austin and Steven Worchel. Chicago, IL: Nelson-Hall.

Tate, Katherine. 1991. "Black Political Participation in the 1984 and 1988 Presidential Elections." *American Political Science Review* 85: 1159–86.

Tate, Katherine. 1994. *From Protest to Politics: The New Black Voters in American Elections*. Cambridge, MA: Harvard University Press.

———. 2003. *Black Faces in the Mirror: African Americans and Their Representatives*. Princeton, NJ: Princeton University Press.

Terkildsen, Nayda. 1993. "When White Voters Evaluate Black Candidates: The Processing Implications of Candidate Skin Color, Prejudice, and Self-Monitoring." *American Journal of Political Science* 37, no. 4: 1032–53.

Terkildsen, Nayda and David F. Damore. 1999. "The Dynamics of Racialized Media Coverage in Congressional Elections." *Journal of Politics* 61: 680–99.

Thurnstrom, Abigail. 2009. *Voting Rights and Wrongs: The Elusive Quest for Racially Fair Elections*. Washington, DC: AEI Press.

Turner, John. 1985. "Social Categorization and the Self-Concept: A Social Cognitive Theory of Group Behavior." *Advances in Group Processes* 2: 77–122.

Valentino, Nicholas A., Vincent L. Hutchings, and Ismail K. White. 2002. "Cues That Matter: How Political Ads Prime Racial Attitudes During Campaigns." *American Political Science Review* 96: 75–90.

Walton Jr., Hanes and Robert C. Smith. 2009. *American Politics and the African American Question for Universal Freedom*, 5th edn). New York: Pearson Longman.

Wilson, David C. 2008. "Prospective Black Presidential Candidates: Can They Win?" *Harvard Journal of African American Public Policy* XIV: 9–25.

Wright-Austin, Sharon and Richard Middleton. 2004. "The Limitations of the Deracialization Concept in the 2001 Los Angeles Mayoral Election." *Political Research Quarterly* 57: 283–93.

Wright, Sharon. 1994. "Electoral and Biracial Coalition: Possible Election Strategy for African American Candidates in Louisville, Kentucky." *Journal of Black Studies* 25: 749–58.

———. 1996. "The Deracialization Strategy and African American Candidates in Memphis Mayoral Elections." In *Race, Politics and Governance in the United States*, edited by Huey L. Perry, 151–64. Gainesville, FL: University Press of Florida.

Zilber, Jeremy and David Niven. 1995. "'Black' versus 'African American:' Are Whites' Political Attitudes Influenced by the Choice of Racial Labels." *Social Science Quarterly* 76: 658–64.

The Foreign Policy Public Opinion Racial Gap in the Obama Era: Exploring the Impact of Political Context

Michael L. Clemons

Introduction

The election of Barack Hussein Obama as the forty-fourth President of the United States raised both hopes and anxieties among American citizens. While many felt that he could somehow bridge the racial divide in America and lead it to an era of post-racialism, others were equally convinced that his presence would only aggravate the problem of race nationally by reinforcing its polarization. In the current era of globalization and proliferating multiculturalism, it is important to delve deeply into this matter. It is evident that Americans and the American political system have responded to President Obama, the nation's first African American[1] president, in a manner that is historically unique. For example, one development on the political landscape is the Tea Party movement of the Republican Party, which has emerged as the embodiment of entrenched White conservative opposition to the policies and programs advanced by the Obama administration. Contrary to the granular thrust of public opinion, the Tea Party's legislative approach has been to oppose reflexively virtually *any* policy position taken by President Obama. In light of the widely held view that the election of Obama would usher in a post-racial America, the following query is in order: How and to what extent has an African American president affected the racial divide in America, particularly in the realm of foreign policy?

Purpose

This article explores the racial gap in foreign policy opinions and the possible impact of a larger political context on this racial gap. Simply put, the foreign policy opinion racial gap is the difference between the attitudes, opinions, and beliefs of Black and White citizens on matters pertaining to foreign policy and global affairs. With the election of President Barack Obama as the first African American head of state, it is prudent to consider the effect of this development on the general patriotism and/or support of African Americans—specifically in regards to U.S. foreign policy. Thus, did the election of Obama (which resulted in a change in descriptive representation at the executive level for African Americans) enlarge the political context of foreign policy making in a manner such that members of this racial group would be more likely than in the past to support U.S. foreign policy? As a corollary, the visual transformation in the context of foreign

25

policy decision-making prompted by the president's skin color, and the growing relevance of multiculturalism suggests the importance of reflecting on whether the opinions and attitudes of African Americans are aligning with those of Whites, or whether the racial divide on matters of American foreign policy persists.

This research is exploratory. It seeks to determine the feasibility of conducting a detailed systematic empirical study and provides a point of departure for the development of the methods needed to investigate the racial divide in American foreign policy attitudes and its context (Babbie 1992, 90–91; Schutt 2001, 12). The study employs existing public opinion research dealing with the foreign policy views of African Americans and Whites. The overarching goal is to investigate the potential for a political context to influence African American foreign policy opinions, and to gauge how it might affect the opinion disparity between African Americans and Whites generally. Specifically of interest are the opinions held by citizens late in the first term of the Bush administration and roughly midway into President Obama's 2008–2012 term. This research considers the possibility that an African American president makes a difference in the foreign policy views that citizens hold, especially Black citizens. Hence, it focuses on how the descriptive representation of African Americans in the Oval Office may affect the racial divide, and whether Obama's election may account for any change that has taken place in the foreign policy views of Americans.

This research is not an attempt to evaluate or assess the quality or results of the foreign policy of the Obama administration. Such a study at present would be premature with only two years completed (at this writing) of at least four, and possibly eight years in the Oval Office. Although this research is at a starting point, it points the way to methods, questions, and in the end, possible answers about the influence of a political context on foreign policy public opinion.

Before proceeding, it is worth noting that the election of an African American president was largely an unanticipated development on the American political landscape. There is no doubt that the conventional wisdom may well have been that the ascendance of a White female to the presidency (possibly Hillary Clinton) would precede the election of an African American male. Perhaps such constrictive popular perspectives help justify the limited motivation of researchers to pursue the subject in earnest. For the most part, despite their value, it appears that mere theoretical and speculative consideration represents to date the nature and extent of the research conducted on the topic.

Methodology

Political scientists have neglected to consider seriously the unique historical and social factors shaping African Americans' foreign policy opinions and behavior. By default, the message imparted to up-and-coming scholars in the field is that African American public opinion is non-existent or insignificant in this arena. Given the state of research and scholarship in the field, I explore the possible effects of the change in political context, stemming from the descriptive representation of African Americans in the American presidency on the contemporary racial divide in foreign policy public opinion in the United States. The article sheds light on the impact of President Barack Obama on the racial divide in American foreign policy opinion. We initially review the history and problems of Black public opinion research. This is followed by an examination of the literature dealing with context and a discussion of how context can influence foreign policy opinions, beliefs, and behavior. In considering whether an African American president makes a difference in the foreign policy beliefs and opinions of Black citizens, we turn our attention to the descriptive results of public opinion polls conducted by the Quinnipiac University Polling Institute and The Pew Research Center for the People and the Press. Given that African Americans comprise a substantial part of President Obama's core constituent base, it is anticipated that his incumbency would affect the political context in a manner that enhances African American patriotism and support of U.S. foreign policy. The article concludes with a discussion of implications and direction for future research. Open to further query, findings from this research may provide a basis that justifies a detailed and systematic empirical investigation of the impact of executive level descriptive representation on foreign policy attitudes and opinions and the foreign policy racial gap.

America's Opinion Racial Divide and the Study of Context

The pattern and trend of Black-White opinion differences have been apparent in political science research since the 1930s when opinion polling for public policy purposes first emerged. While the mere presence of the race gap is itself intriguing, the more complex matter deals with the underlying factors and conditions impelling the divergence of Black and White opinions. In this section, we present and discuss the scholarly research dealing with the racial divide. The research on political context is also examined, and we speculate on the question of the connection between the political context of race and public opinion.

The opinions, attitudes, and beliefs of most Americans are attributable not to a single societal force, but rather are interlaced with individuals' day-to-day lives. This suggests that demographics and environment play an immense role in attitudinal formation. While the history of racial politics in the United States has led to making race a formative variable, Kinder and Winter (2001) point out that the American public opinion divide are in actuality two racial divides—one based on the ideal of racial equality, the other on the principle of social welfare. While social class is more important as a factor for Whites, in the case of Blacks, racial identification is the most salient factor. Hence, "On issues like affirmative action, blacks tend to be concerned with political principles like equal opportunity, while whites tend to be concerned with big government; blacks tend to express group solidarity, while whites tend to express resentment" (Carroll 2005, 97).

Nature of the Foreign Policy Racial Divide

In foreign policy opinion research, race has been one of the most consistent correlates of American attitudes toward foreign policy, especially in connection with matters concerning the use of force abroad. However, other variables such as class, education, income, and views about democratic values confound the situation, rendering it difficult to ascertain how much race actually accounts for citizens' attitudes (Hero 1959; McClosky 1964; Wittkopf 1990, 41, 44; Wittkopf 1995, 14). Bobo and Lacari (1989), for example, found education to be strongly related with tolerance. It has also been shown, for example, that levels of education are associated with support for diverse racial and ethnic groups. Nevertheless, despite the lack of consensus among researchers regarding the degree to which race influences the opinions of citizens, it is clear in contemporary circumstances that race plays a growing role in foreign affairs and foreign policy making (Holsti 2004).

During the latter years of the twentieth century, the opinions of Blacks and Whites were consistently divergent on the issue of support for war (Carroll 2005, 1). With the outbreak of the Gulf War in 1990, the racial disparity between opinions held by Blacks and Whites persisted, although in some instances, the gap widened. A Gallup Organization survey of July 21, 1991 showed that only 37 percent of African Americans compared to 78 percent of Whites, in retrospect, approved of U.S. intervention in Kuwait during the Persian Gulf War. Interestingly, the proportion of non-Whites (also non-Blacks) registering retrospective support for the intervention in Kuwait "to drive the Iraqi troops out" was 46 percent: a level of support more closely aligned with that registered by African Americans (37 percent) (Holsti 2004, 229). This example illustrates the racial shakeout of Americans' support for the use of force abroad. The alignment of African Americans and other non-Whites may reinforce the notion that White Americans view the world and respond on the global stage in a manner differently from people of color and other cultural groups. In the case of the Gulf War, Smith and Seltzer (2000) explain that Blacks'

> . . . ambivalent opposition is rooted in historical and structural forces that allow the black community to resist, more so than whites, mainstream, elite framing of foreign policy issues. Historically, from the Mexican American War to the Vietnam War, blacks have tended to oppose American wars in general and those wars in the Third World in particular. The latter tendency represents a kind of Third World solidarity with people of color; what one scholar referred to more broadly as an Afro-Centric perspective (58).

Hence, the endurance of the racial divide seems to lend credence to the argument that the African American experience emanates from a unique vantage point. Indeed, historical and structural conditions have facilitated the creation of a Black global framework that filters and conditions views and interpretations of Western, and U.S. foreign policy decisions outside of a mainstream or consensus opinion.

It was during the 1960s that the racial divide was firmly established. In the aftermath of the civil rights movement, the racial divide became even more entrenched. Recently, even absent the salience of race in public discourse, the racial gap appears to have remained deeply entrenched in foreign affairs despite the fact that Americans all too often are depicted as uninterested, alienated, and too preoccupied with day-to-day life to be concerned about foreign affairs. Indeed, given the advantages of technology and communication advances, it may be that Americans are today more engaged than ever in foreign affairs. However, this assertion requires further investigation.

While there may be an historical and empirical basis for a claim to the contrary, it is evident that certain foreign policy decisions (e.g., the decision to engage troops in combat on foreign soil) can stimulate nationalism, patriotism, and unity among citizens. However, this is not necessarily the case with respect to Black Americans in the post 9/11 era. In this period there is evidence that suggests race is congealing as an important source of differences among Americans on foreign policy matters. For example, the National Election Study and the Gallup Polls found that the racial gap persisted on the issues of military operations being conducted in the Persian Gulf War (by 31 percentage points) and in Serbia (by 19 percentage points) (Erikson and Tedin 2001). Another study which tested the effect of 9/11 on the racial divide on the issue of support for war reported that "The racial divide in relation to 9/11 is as large as or larger than it has been in our nation's history even after controlling for varying levels of income and education among cognitively engaged individuals" (Carroll 2005, 107). Surveys revealed further that while there were moderate differences among Whites and Asians and Latinos, the magnitude of difference between Whites and African Americans "can only be described as enormous" (Holsti 2007, 288). This discussion leads us to pose the following question: Why does the racial divide persist in the foreign policy opinions of African Americans and Whites?

One can begin to discuss the racial gap in foreign policy public opinion initially by viewing it in light of structural considerations. For example, during much of the nation's history, the powerful elites who often have been stakeholders in foreign policy decisions have also controlled the foreign policy-making process itself. Foreign policy-making has been practically the exclusive domain of White male elites. As such, it has generally been understood that non-Whites as well as women were non-essential to the process, and in the case of African Americans, their opinions were neither sought nor acknowledged (Skinner 1992).

Another way in which structural factors manifest themselves in foreign affairs is in the global proliferation of cultural connectedness. Presently, foreign policy decision-making collides with an expanding global multiculturalism—one that provides a vehicle for citizens' informal interaction with relevant cultural diasporas. This dynamic helps to shape foreign policy making. Technology's rapid proliferation, especially through computers and satellite communication, plays a major role in the building of cultural and political bridges between peoples across the globe who hitherto had only a vague sense of their shared identities. The spread of multiculturalism, through modern technology, facilitates the discovery of the common threads of history, the contemporary circumstances of life, and the policy alternatives that reflect greater desire for inclusiveness.

Nevertheless, for the foreseeable future, White elites will control the reins of foreign policy decision-making. However, it is clear that the foreign policy making process is both horizontal and vertical, and that non-elite social groups can potentially exert enormous pressure on the foreign policy-making apparatus. Today racial and cultural groups can be potential power brokers even in limited ways. Given this circumstance, it is not surprising that the domestic social conditions associated with race have generated deep divisions in the attitudes of African Americans and Whites, not only in the domestic political arena (Erikson et al. 1991, 177–81), but also in the field of foreign affairs.

Opinion Research and the Study of Context

The shortcomings of the opinion research on African Americans are threefold: (1) methodological negligence on the part of some researchers, (2) one-sided ideological treatment of research dealing with race and public opinion, and (3) the limited quantity and breadth of work on the subject. It is not surprising, therefore, that the changing racial and multicultural context of U.S. foreign policy making has not received greater attention as a matter worthy of research. The study of foreign policy making in the discipline of political science traditionally has emphasized the dominant role that governmental institutions and elites play over interest groups and individual citizens. However, the emerging demographic realities of the twenty-first century necessitate that American foreign policy making be studied in light of globalism and multiculturalism.

Some of the early cross-sectional research on citizen participation conducted in the 1970s and 1980s, revealed Blacks were participating at higher rates than Whites (Guterbock and London 1983; Shingles 1981; Verba and Nie 1972; Welch and Secret 1981). Later work suggested, however, that these earlier findings reflected the tumultuous era of Black Power. Specifically, researchers began to show that when taking into account resources and socioeconomic status (SES), no differences in participation were detected between Blacks and Whites (Bobo and Gilliam 1990; Leighly and Veditz 1999; Verba et al. 1993).

Studies on context go beyond mere explanation of political behavior by seeking insight into how political behavior unfolds in a particular milieu. Research on context has examined political behavior within the framework of urban sprawl (Humphries 2001; Oliver 1999), political party mobilization (Gershetenson 2002; Hill and Leighley 1993; Rosenstone and Hansen 1993), social networks (Cho 2003; Huckfeldt 1979), anti-terrorism policies (Cho et al. 2006) and descriptive representation[2] (Bobo and Gilliam 1990; Gay 2001, 2002; Griffin and Kean 2006; Lawless 2004). Context, which is comprised of political, social, economic, cultural, or some combination of these factors, shapes opinions and attitudes, which in turn help direct citizen's political behavior. In the case of African Americans, political context, reflected through descriptive representation has been shown to influence voting behavior (Tate 1993; Walton 2004). Although an individual's voting behavior may well be indicative of her/his foreign policy preferences, it is quite likely that much more can be learned by examining how context may directly affect foreign policy attitudes and opinions.

In foreign affairs a number of variables have been shown to be associated with, but not necessarily causally linked to citizens' foreign policy attitudes and opinions. There have been few opportunities to assess the impact of context. Even the successive ascendancies of Colin Powell and Condoleezza Rice to the position of secretary of state failed to stimulate substantial inquiry among scholars regarding the influence of descriptive representation (i.e., African American) on American's foreign policy attitudes, beliefs, and opinions. This exploration turns our attention to the matter of how political context, reflected through the descriptive representation of African Americans at the highest level of the foreign policy making apparatus, affects the foreign policy views of Blacks and Whites.

Context helps shape the nature and quality of Black political behavior and, arguably, vice versa. Scholars generally have focused on context as it relates to mobilization, elections, voter turnout, and political empowerment. It has been demonstrated, for example, that ballot referenda, government budgeting, election cycles, and congressional activity influence participation due to the active efforts of political elites to attract individuals to their policy positions (Rosenstone and Hansen 1993). Studies of voter turnout and non-electoral campaign participation have also found that such participation is highest when the political parties present voters with clearly distinctive competitive platforms (Corder and Wolbrecht 2006; Gershtenson 2002; Hill and Leighley 1993, 1996). While these studies provide valuable insight into how identity forms political context, the most demonstrative findings in this regard are in the empowerment research. Works concentrating on empowerment point out that descriptive representation signals to constituents that government will be more responsive. The perceived opportunity for improved governmental response on important and relevant matters translates into greater trust, efficacy, and knowledge on the part of constituents (Bobo and Gilliam 1990).

As a political variable, "context" is interesting in that it can operate as both an independent and dependent variable. "Political context" has been defined as "…a thesis which postulates that political behavior at either the individual or the group level is not independent of the political environment (a particular time period and a particular place) in which it occurs" (Walton 1997, 7). Milbrath and Gael (1977) appear to see political context and environmental factors as virtually the same. They assert that there are factors or environmental considerations that facilitate a human behavior separate and apart from the individual's specific characteristics. They observe that, "There are a variety of contextual or environmental variables that could affect political participation . . . the cultural milieu, the social-structural character of the community, and the political setting" (Milbrath and Gael 1977, 123). It is the "cultural milieu" which directs an individual's "cognitive engagement." Cognitive engagement is the attention an individual gives to those things that comprise the relevant environment (Shally 1995).

In light of the present discussion, this question can be raised: Does the presence of an African American president alter the foreign policy making context in a manner that increases African Americans' support of the system and, if so, to what extent? This matter has been addressed in general reference to Black political participation as there is a parallel track of research that has gradually turned its attention to the serious study of African American voting behavior and the effects of context on that behavior. One of the key findings reported in the literature is that the presidential campaigns of Jesse L. Jackson, a key contender in the 1984 and 1988 Democratic primaries, led to a heightened interest and increased Black voting behavior. The work of Katherine Tate (1993) and others was at the forefront of a wave of research analyzing Black voting participation and demonstrating the connection between said behavior and context. In the field of foreign affairs, scant attention has been given to Black support for foreign policies, and as a consequence, there is slight analysis which applies the concept of context to the evolving attitudes of Black Americans on foreign affairs issues. Hence, one can only speculate about whether Barack Obama's occupancy of the oval office, like Jackson's serious pursuit of the office, has had an impact on shaping Black attitudes and even furthering the racial divide.

Analysis and Discussion

The ballyhoo surrounding Barack Obama had much to do with the belief of many Americans that his presidential victory would signify the decline of race as a salient feature in American society. This view, however, runs largely contrary to the literature that suggests that race remains a critical variable in American politics. This contrast gives rise to the following broad question: Does political context, as reflected by the descriptive representation of African Americans in the presidency since the election of President Obama, affect the opinions of Americans in a manner that fuels the foreign policy racial gap? To initially explore this matter, cross-racial comparisons are made based on national polls conducted by the Quinnipiac University Polling Institute (QUPI) on September 17, 2003 and April 22, 2010.[3] This starting point allows us to establish the presence and direction of the foreign policy racial gap on the issues selected. Specifically, we examine Black and White survey participants' approval of the president's: (1) handling of foreign policy generally, (2) his handling of terrorism, and (3) his handling of the Middle East situation between the Palestinians and Israelis. These items are our focus because of the understanding of their being mainstream foreign policy issues and because the items allow for systematic analysis since they are contained in the QUPI survey over the period covering two presidential administrations, of George Bush and Barak Obama. Previous research leads to the following expectations: (1) a foreign policy racial gap (in reference to the items examined) will be present during both the Bush and Obama terms and (2) the foreign policy racial gap will show a declining trend from 2003 (Bush) to 2010 (Obama); that is, the gap between Whites and Blacks will diminish. At issue is whether the descriptive representation of African Americans at the highest level of U.S. foreign policy making affects the way in which Americans, Black and White, view foreign policy decisions, consequently affecting the foreign policy racial gap.

Along with the results of the Quinnipiac University polls, the results of surveys conducted between 1999 and 2009 by the Pew Research Center for the People and the Press[4] spanning the administrations of Bush and Obama, are presented and discussed. These results summarize the responses of Black and White citizens to the declaration that they would "fight for our country, even when wrong." The significance of this query is that it provides an indication or measure of respondents' *unconditional commitment* to defending the United States. Consideration of this question across presidential administrations can provide significant insight into the connection between political context and the importance of descriptive representation on the foreign policy racial divide.

Handling of Foreign Policy

In national polls dealing with foreign affairs, frequently a representative cross-section of respondents is asked whether respondents approve or disapprove of the way the president is handling foreign policy. Two years following the attack on New York City's World Trade Center and the Pentagon on September 11, 2001, a poll conducted by Quinnipiac University in September 2003 showed that respondents' support for President George W. Bush's "handling" of foreign policy (49 percent) only surpassed by a few percentage points survey results indicating a lack of approval (44 percent). (See Table 1) As shown in Table 1, almost seven years later Bush's Black successor garnered similar levels of approval and disapproval for his handing of foreign policy (48 percent and 42 percent, respectively). However, with respect to partisan differences, the 2010 survey revealed a gulf between Democrats (63 percent) and Republicans (16 percent) on President Obama's handling of foreign policy, comparable to that shown by the 2003 survey with regard to President Bush. (Table 1) Moreover, African Americans' approval of Obama's handling of foreign policy (82 percent) in April 2010 was double that for Whites (41 percent). These findings are consistent with the expectation that Blacks and Whites continue to have a difference of opinion when it comes to the president's handling of foreign policy. However, the 2010 survey indicates that while African Americans, like Democrats, enthusiastically support President Obama's handling of foreign policy, they were not as supportive of Bush's handling of foreign policy in 2003.

Table 1 also compares the racial gaps occurring in 2003 (22 percent) and 2010 (41 percent). The racial gap is calculated by subtracting the smallest percentage of

Table 1.
Quinnipiac University Polling Institute National Survey Results for Barack Obama
(April 22, 2010) and George W. Bush (September 17, 2003): Handling of Foreign Policy

| | % Approve | | % Disapprove | |
	Bush (2003)	Obama (2010)	Bush (2003)	Obama (2008)
Total	49	48	44	42
African American	23	82	73	10
White	55	41	38	48
Democrat	22	63	71	26
Republican	83	16	13	73
	Racial Gap			
	Bush (2003)	Obama (2010)	% Change	
Aft-Amer-White	32 pts	41 pts	+9	

Source: Quinnipiac University Polling Institute, National Surveys, Hamden, CT, September 17, 2003 and April 22, 2010.

presidential approval by African Americans or Whites from the largest percentage of approval by African Americans or Whites. The change for the period in the opinion difference of Blacks and Whites concerning the president's handling of foreign policy was +9 percentage points. This increase may be due to the simultaneous overwhelming support of President Obama by African Americans, and the defection of some Whites who had previously supported the president's handling of foreign policy. The high level of Black support enjoyed by Obama is indicative of his racial connection with African Americans, despite his steadfast maintenance of a racially neutral public posture.

On the other hand, the fact that Obama is Black may have also prompted some Whites to defect from supporting the president's handling of foreign policy. Notwithstanding Republican partisanship, the relatively low level of White approval of Obama's handling of foreign policy in 2010 is contrary to the reality that he has continued many of the policies of the preceding administration of George W. Bush. While this analysis speaks only to the presence and magnitude the racial gap from Bush to Obama, it would be interesting to investigate more precisely how much of Obama's rating on the handling of foreign policy is accounted for by race. Obama's election to the presidency may have prompted, on the part of both African American leaders and the rank-and-file, greater engagement as well as increased scrutiny of U.S. foreign policy. However, his presence not only likely stimulated Blacks' support of the handling of a president's foreign policy, it may have activated some Whites with a genuine substantive disagreement, and others with superficial feelings of racial antagonisms against Obama to register dissatisfaction with his policies.

Handling of Terrorism

Despite the lack of success of transnational operatives in attacking the United States in the post 9/11 era, terrorism response and prevention was a front burner issue throughout the 2008 presidential race. The issue of terrorism, to a large degree, unfolded as a make or break issue for presidential candidates. Barack Obama's opposition on the war in Iraq in the U.S. Senate served him well during his presidential campaign. His dissent highlighted his independence and strength as a politician, and was convincing evidence that early on in this upheaval in the Middle East he had the "good judgment" and "resolve," to stand firmly against the political grain of U.S. military intervention in Iraq.

In 2003 and 2010, the Quinnipiac University poll queried respondents about the president's "handling of terrorism." The 2003 results revealed strong approval of the way Bush was handling the matter (56 percent see Table 2). In April 2010, a poll revealed that 49 percent of the respondents approved Obama's handling of terrorism (see Table 2). However, both polls reveal a startling divide between Blacks and Whites. The 2003 poll showed that while 61 percent of Whites approved of Bush's handling of terrorism, only 32 percent of Blacks approved. In 2010, an overwhelming 81 percent of African Americans expressed approval of Obama's handling of terrorism, in contrast to 41 percent of Whites.

Thus, White approval of Bush's handling of terrorism was about twice that of Blacks. On the other hand, African American's approval of Obama's handling of terrorism was about twice that for Whites. Moreover, the poll revealed vast differences in citizens' approval of the president's handling of terrorism on a partisan basis. While Republicans expressed virtually overwhelming approval of Bush's handling of terrorism (86 percent), Democrats did not express similar levels of approval (30 percent) The percentage of Republicans approving of Obama's handling of terrorism was 22 percent, 8 percentage points lower than Democrats' approval of Bush.

Comparison of the racial gaps occurring in 2003 (31 percent) and 2010 (40 percent) reveal an increase of 9 percentage points in the difference of the opinions of Blacks and Whites regarding the president's handling of terrorism between 2003 and 2010. The

Table 2.
Quinnipiac University Polling Institute National Survey Results for Barack Obama (April 22, 2010) and George W. Bush (September 17, 2003): Handling of Terrorism

	% Approve		% Disapprove	
	Bush	**Obama**	**Bush**	**Obama**
Total	56	49	38	41
African American	32	81	63	13
White	61	41	33	47
Democrat	30	80	63	13
Republican	86	22	11	70
	Racial Gap			
	Bush	**Obama**	**% Change**	
Aft-Amer-White	31 pts	40 pts	+9	

Source: Quinnipiac University Polling Institute, National Surveys, Hamden, CT, September 17, 2003 and April 22, 2010.

relatively low approval by Whites of Obama's handling of terrorism combined with the extraordinary level of approval of African Americans likely contributed to the increase in the racial gap on the matter of the handling of terrorism between 2003 and 2010.

Handling of the Israeli-Palestinian Situation

A challenging and persistent foreign policy issue plaguing U.S. presidents since the founding of the state of Israel in 1948 has been efforts at achieving peaceful relations between the Israeli and the Palestinian peoples. Moreover, the erosion of Black-Jewish relations over the past two decades has further fueled the complexity of the situation. Conflict over a domestic issues such as affirmative action, linked to an international one, such as the rights of the Palestinians to a Palestinian state, a position supported by a sizeable percentage of African Americans since at least the 1970s, likely affects the political context within which Obama's Middle East foreign policy will be judged. (Figures such as W.E.B. Du Bois incidentally supported Palestinian rights.) In 2003, a Quinnipiac University poll found that 41 percent approved of President Bush's handling of the Israel-Palestinian situation, while 39 percent disapproved. On a partisan basis, 63 percent of Republicans compared to 25 percent of Democrats approved. In 2010, only 35 percent of the total respondents in the Quinnipiac poll reported approval of President Obama's handling of the Israel-Palestinian matter (See Table 3). However, 68 percent of African Americans registered their support for his handling of the issue, a level almost twice that for respondents overall and well more than double that for Whites. In terms of party identification, while 59 percent of Democrats approved, only 15 percent of Republicans concurred. Given the circumstances of domestic politics and the rift in African American–Jewish relations, it is not surprising that on the matter of Obama's handling of the Israel-Palestinian issue that there is a persistent and substantial racial divide.

Table 3.
Quinnipiac University Polling Institute National Survey Results for Barack Obama (April 22, 2010) and George W. Bush (September 17, 2003): Handling of Israel–Palestinian Situation

	% Approve		% Disapprove	
	Bush	**Obama**	**Bush**	**Obama**
Total	41	35	39	44
African American	24	68	58	20
White	44	30	37	49
Democrat	25	59	55	19
Republican	63	15	18	68
Racial Gap	**Bush (2003)**	**Obama (2010)**	**% Change**	
Aft-Amer-White	20 pts	38 pts	+18	

Source: Quinnipiac University Polling Institute, National Surveys, Hamden, CT, September 17, 2003 and April 22, 2010.

The findings presented above based on selected items in public opinion surveys conducted by Quinnipiac University Polling Institute show that significant differences (and in some cases, the quite large differences) endure among Blacks and Whites on key foreign policy questions. Consistent with results presented and discussed on the two previous survey questions, between 2003 and 2010 there was a widening of the racial gap from 20 percentage points to 38 percentage points. These findings run counter to the notion of post-racialism, suggesting the possibility of heightened racial polarization during the Obama presidency. The increase in the Black-White racial gap (18 percentage points) between 2003 and 2011 may be due to Blacks' low approval of Bush's policies in 2003 and their unusually strong support of President Obama's policies in 2010. Next, we consider the possibility that Obama's election to the presidency has profoundly changed the political context of foreign policy making and consequently Black attitudes and opinions.

Political Context and African American Opinion

The Political Values and Core Attitudes survey, conducted since 1987 by The Pew Research Center for the People and the Press, have gauged Americans' unconditional national commitment by asking respondents whether they would "fight for the country, even when wrong." This query can yield important insights into the quality and nature of citizens' support of government, and an understanding of the depth of their patriotic commitment. Table 4 reports the percentage of Blacks and Whites responding for selected years between 1999 and 2009 to this question in the survey. While the trend generally indicates stability overtime both for respondents overall and Whites, there is a different longitudinal pattern revealed for Black respondents. Although the effect of partisanship is difficult to sort out based on the data presented in Table 4, it is evident that from 2007 to 2009 a "change" took place among Black Americans in reference to their willingness to participate unconditionally in the country's application of force and participation in war. It is noteworthy that the racial divide on this question in 1999 under White Democratic President Bill Clinton was 6 percentage points. Ten years later, with the first African

Table 4.
Percentage of Respondents Who Agree with the Statement "Fight for Our Country, Even When Wrong"

	1999 (%)	2002 (%)	2003 (%)	2007 (%)	2009 (%)	2007–2009 (% Change)
Total	49	52	52	50	53	+3
White	51	55	54	52	55	+3
Black	45	42	29	30	45	+15
Racial gap[a]	6	13	25	22	10	

Source: Adapted from The Pew Research Center for the People and the Press, Section 6, Foreign Policy and Global Engagement, http://people-press.org/2009/05/21/section-6-foreign-policy-and-global-engagement/.

[a]The racial gap is calculated by subtracting the percentage of Blacks in agreement from the percentage of Whites in agreement.

American in the White House there was a 10-percentage point difference in the racial gap, an increase of 4 percentage points. This may suggest that some Whites who previously agreed with the statement may have defected from their prior support of the president. The table also shows that in 2003 during the administration of George W. Bush, that the racial gap was its highest during the ten-year period (25 percentage points). According to survey findings, five years later in 2007, the racial gap narrowed by only three percentage points (from 25 percentage points in 2003 to 22 in 2007). However, the overall pattern of responses for the period is stable, ranging from a low of 49 percent in 1999 to a high of 53 percent in 2009. A similar pattern is observed for Whites , with a low of 51 percent agreeing with the statement "fight for our country, even when wrong" in 1999, compared to a high of 55 percent in both 2002 and 2009. In contrast, the percentage of African Americans who agree with the statement has been more volatile, ranging from a low of 39 percent in 2003 to a high of 45 percent in both 1999 and 2009, each of which are years when a Democrat occupied the White House. The percentage of African Americans agreeing with the statement "fight for our country, right or wrong" increased by 15 percentage points between 2007 and 2009—from 30 percent to 45percent. It may be that Obama's 2008 election victory positively affected the willingness of African Americans to unconditionally fight for the United States. Indeed, it is reasonable to assume that Obama's election had a positive impact on the experiential lens of African Americans due to the pride they felt because of his victory. Continuing with this interpretation, Obama's rise to power enhanced the Black community's self-esteem. Partisanship and racial consciousness, as variables, both likely help explain the strong increase in Black support of the notion that one ought to fight for his or her country, even if he or she feels the country is wrong.

Conclusion and Implications

The purpose of this exploratory study has been to investigate the foreign policy opinions held by Black and White Americans toward selected issues dealing with the international arena. While the results of this exploratory study are inconclusive, several key points can be distilled which have important implications for the direction of future research.

The results of the Quinnipiac University Polling Institute (QUPI) and the Pew surveys are mixed in regards to signaling Obama's impact on the foreign policy racial gap. While the QUPI surveys point to a widening of the foreign policy racial gap, the Pew surveys suggest that the racial gap closed significantly (declined from a 25 percentage point difference in 2003 to a 10 percentage point difference in 2009) in reference to respondents agreeing with the statement, "fight for our country, even when wrong." Despite these mixed findings, it appears that race remains a salient factor shaping the opinions of Black and White Americans, and that the jury is still out on the question of whether the racial divide is still with us in the era of Obama.

This study suggests that the presence of President Obama has positively affected African Americans' view of how foreign policy is generally handled, the handling of terrorism, and the situation between Israel and the Palestinians. In addition, the five-year trend data from the Pew studies point to the possibility that, since becoming president of the United States, Obama has changed or is changing the context of U.S. foreign policy making. His presence appears to have stimulated African American support of U.S. foreign policy even to the point in situations where the country is deemed incorrect, African Americans support the president's policies and approach. On the other hand, the data also suggest that President Obama might also affect Whites in a manner that increases racial polarization, and consequently the foreign policy racial gap. For example, some Whites, perhaps those who would self-identify as "independent," may have defected from their previous inclination to support the president's work in the foreign policy field, thus facilitating maintenance, if not the widening of, the foreign policy racial gap. If Black support of the president increases and there is a simultaneous erosion of White support of the president, then the likelihood is that the disparity regarding the foreign policy is not only a political party gap, but also a racial gap.

While the findings and implications of this research are preliminary, further systematic empirical inquiry is warranted to understand more fully the role of descriptive representation in the formulation and support of American foreign policy and the influence of political context on foreign policy opinions and the consequential racial gap. Clearly, there is a need for further research concerning the effect of race and the impact of the Obama presidency. There would also be considerable utility in examining whether the descriptive representation of African Americans provided by Colin Powell and later Condoleezza Rice had an effect on African Americans similar to that of Obama, despite their Republican partisanship, as well as a measure of the means by which African Americans parse racial membership in the presence of the party identification of the foreign policy official. Future research should concentrate more holistically on high level Black foreign policy actors, and their role and impact in shaping the political context, and consequently the opinions, attitudes, beliefs, and behaviors of Whites, Blacks, and other non-White racial subgroups in the foreign policy-making process.

Acknowledgments: An earlier version of this paper was presented at the March 16–19, 2011 annual meeting of the National Conference of Black Political Scientists, Raleigh, North Carolina. The author would like to extend his gratitude to Professor William H.L. Dorsey for his careful reading of the manuscript.

Notes

1. The terms "Black" and "African American" are used interchangeably in this article.
2. For a full discussion of descriptive representation see Paula McClain and Joseph Stewart (2002) and Charles Mennifield (2001). Although descriptive representation as a single factor is insufficient for bringing about political and social parity of racial and ethnic groups, scholars acknowledge that it is a positive factor in the achievement of group empowerment (Barreto et al. 2004; Button et al. 1998; Mansbridge 1999).
3. This research makes cross-racial comparisons based on descriptive results from national polls conducted by the Quinnipiac University Polling Institute (QUPI) on September 17, 2003 and April 22, 2010. A national poll released on September 17, 2003 was carried out from September 11–15. For purposes of the survey 1,228 registered voters nationwide were contacted, with a margin of error of ±2.8 percent. The survey includes 466 Democrats with a margin of error of ±4.5 percent. The descriptive results of the QUPI poll released on April 22, 2010 are also employed in this research. For this survey, from April 14–19, Quinnipiac University surveyed 1,930 registered voters nationwide with a margin of error of ±2.2 percentage points.
4. Since 1987, the Pew Research Center for the People and the Press has conducted surveys to track the values and opinions of Americans. The sampling error for a typical Pew Research Center for the People and the Press national survey of 1,500 completed interviews is ±3 percentage points with a 95 percent confidence interval. This means that in 95 out of every 100 samples of the same size and type, the results we obtain would vary by no more than ±3 percentage points from the result we would get if we could interview every member of the population.

References

Anderson, Carol. 2003. *Eyes Off the Prize: The United Nations and the African American Struggle for Human Rights, 1944–1955*. Cambridge: Cambridge University Press.

Babbie, Earl. 1992. *The Practice of Social Research*, 6th edn. Belmont, CA: Wadsworth Publishing Company.

Barreto, Matt A., Gary M. Segura, and Nathan D. Woods. 2004. "The Mobilizing Effect of Majority-Minority Districts on Latino Turnout." *American Political Science Review* 98, no. 1 (February): 65–75.

Bobo, Lawrence, and Franklin Gilliam. 1990. "Race, Sociopolitical Participation, and Black Political Empowerment." *American Political Science Review* 84: 377–97.

Bobo, Lawrence and Frederick C. Licari. 1989. "Education and Political Tolerance: Testing the Effects of cognitive Sophistication and Target Group Affect." *Public Opinion Quarterly* 53, no. 3: 285–308.

Borstlemann, Thomas. 2001. *The Cold War and the Color Line: American Race Relations in the Global Arena*. Cambridge, MA: Harvard University Press.

Button, James, Scott Richards, and Evelyn Bethune. 1998. "A Look at the Second Generation of Black Elected Officials in Florida." *State and Local Government Review* 30, no. 3 (Fall): 181–189.

Carroll, Bruce A. 2005. "Spanning the Racial Divide in American Public Opinion: Post-September 11." *Politics & Policy* 33, no. 1: 94–112.

Corder, J. Kevin and Christina Wolbrecht. 2006. "Political Context and the Turnout of New Women Voters after Suffrage." *Journal of Politics* 68: 38–49.

Dudziak, Mary L. 2000. "Cold War Civil Rights: Race and the Image of American Democracy," In *Politics and Society in Twentieth Century America*, edited by William Chafe, Gary Gerstle, and Linda Gordon. Princeton, NJ: Princeton University Press.

Erikson, Robert S., Norman R. Luttbeg, and Kent L. Tedin. 1991. *American Public Opinion*, 4th edn. New York: Macmillan Publishing Company.

Erikson, Robert S. and Kent L. Tedin. 2001. *American Public Opinion*, 6th edn. New York: Longman.

Gay, Claudine. 2001. "The Effect of Black Congressional Representation on Political Participation." *American Political Science Review* 95: 589–617.

———. 2002. "Spirals of Trust? The Effect of Descriptive Representation on the Relationship between Citizens and their Government." *American Journal of Political Science* 46: 717–32.

Gershtenson, Joseph. 2002. "Partisanship and Participation in Political Campaign Activities, 1952–1996." *Political Research Quarterly* 55: 687–714.

Guterbock, Thomas M. and Bruce London. 1983. "Race, Political Orientation, and Participation: An Empirical Test of Four Competing Theories." *American Sociological Review* 48: 439–53.

Hero, Alfred O., Jr. 1959. *Americans in World Affairs*. Boston, MA: World Peace Foundation.

Hill, Kim Quaile and Jan E. Leighley. 1993. "Party Ideology, Organization, and Competitiveness as Mobilizing Forces in Gubernatorial Elections." *American Journal of Political Science* 37: 1158–78.

———. 1996. "Political Parties and Class Mobilization in Contemporary United States Elections." *American Journal of Political Science* 40: 787–804.

Holsti, Ole R. 2004. *Public Opinion and American Foreign Policy*, Revised edn. Ann Arbor, MI: The University of Michigan Press.

Krenn, Michael L. 1999. *Black Diplomacy: African Americans and the State Department, 1945–1969*. Armonk, NY: M.E. Sharpe.

Kinder, Donald R. and Nicholas Winter. 2001. "Exploring the Racial Divide: Blacks, Whites, and Opinion on National Policy." *American Journal of Political Science* 45, no. 2: 439–53.

Kubic, Micah W. 2009. "A Different Vision: African-Americans, America as Superpower, and Presidential Politics." Paper presented at the annual meeting of the Northeastern Political Science Association, November 19.

Leighley, Jan E. and Arnold Vedlitz. 1999. "Race, Ethnicity, and Political Participation: Competing Models and Contrasting Explanations." *Journal of Politics* 61: 1092–114.

Mansbridge, Jane. 1999. "Should Blacks Represent Blacks and Women Represent Women? A Contingent 'Yes'." *Journal of Politics* 61 (August): 628–57.

McClain, Paula D and Joseph Stewart, Jr. 2002. *"Can We All Get Along?" Racial and Ethnic Minorities in American Politics*, 3rd edn. Boulder, CO: Westview Press.

Menifield, Charles E., ed. 2001. *Representation of Minority Groups in the U.S.: Implications for the Twenty-First Century*. Lanham, MD: Austin & Winfield Publishers.

Milbrath, Lester and M. L. Gael. 1977. *Political Participation*, 2nd edn. Chicago, IL: Rand McNally.

Myrdal, Gunnar. 1962. *An American Dilemma: The Negro Problem and Modern Democracy*. New York: Harper and Row.

Rosenstone, Steven J. and John Mark Hansen. 1993. *Mobilization, Participation, and Democracy.* New York: Macmillan.

Schutt, Russell K. 2001. *Investigating the Social World: The Process and Practice of Research*, 3rd edn. Thousand Oaks, CA: Pine Forge Press.

Shalley, Christina E. 1995. "Effects of Coaction, Expected Evaluation, and Goal Setting on Creativity and Productivity." *The Academy of Management Journal* 38, no. 2: 483–503.

Shingles, Richard D. 1981. "Black Consciousness and Political Participation: The Missing Link." *American Political Science Review* 75: 76–91.

Sigelman, Lee and Susan Welch. 1994. *Black Americans' Views of Racial Inequality: The Dream Deferred.* New York: Cambridge University Press.

Skinner, Elliott P. 1992. *African Americans and U.S. Policy toward Africa, 1850–1924: In Defense of Black Nationality.* Washington: Howard University Press.

Smith, Robert C. and Richard Seltzer. 2000. *Contemporary Controversies and the American Racial Divide.* New York: Rowman & Littlefield Publishers, Inc.

Tate, Katherine. 1993. *From Protest to Politics: The New Black Voters in American Elections.* New York: Russell Sage Foundation.

Verba, Sidney and Norman Nie. 1972. *Participation in America.* New York: Harper and Row.

Walton, Jr. Hanes. 1997. *African American Power and Politics: The Political Context Variable.* New York: Columbia University Press.

———. 2004. "African American Public Opinion, White Scholars, and a Neo-Conservative Political Context." *Du Bois Review* 1, no. 2: 393–97.

Walton, Jr. Hanes and Robert C. Smith. 2006. *American Politics and the African American Quest for Universal Freedom*, 3rd edn. New York: Pearson Longman.

Welch, Susan and Philip Secret. 1981. "Sex, Race and Political Participation." *Western Political Quarterly* 34: 5–16.

Wittkopf, Eugene R. 1990. *Faces of Internationalism: Public Opinion and American Foreign Policy.* Durham, NC: Duke University Press.

———. 1995. "The Faces of Internationalism Revisited: Paper presented at the annual meeting of the American Political Science Association, Chicago, August 31–September 3.

Opinion Polling Sources

Quinnipiac University Polling Institute, 2003. National Surveys. Hamden, CT, September 3.

———. 2003. National Surveys. Hamden, CT, April 22, 2010.

The Pew Center for the People and the Press. 2009. *Trends in Political Values and Core Attitudes: 1987–2009.* Section 6, Foreign Policy and Global Engagement. May 21, http://people-press.org/report/?pageid=1521.

The United Nations and the African American Presence: From Ralph Bunche to Susan Rice

Lorenzo Morris

Assumptions and Expectations

The ideal American ambassador is "the invisible man or woman," who conforms to the policy directives of the White House while refining them, adjusting them, and occasionally correcting misconceptions but consistently minimizing personal visibility. Where visible he/she should be seen as the spokesperson in a specific issue area or agency while any role in policy formulation should be invisible to the public. For African American U.N. ambassadors in the past, however, this has proven to be a near impossibility. At most, these ambassadors could only hope to escape the defining pressures of race relations by sinking into the kind of active inertia bemoaned by Ralph Ellison in *The Invisible Man*. In this case, that means minimizing personal initiative and denying or rejecting other initiatives that may involve race in order to avoid the unwarranted assumption of a racial factor. In avoiding such initiatives they are most likely to be seen as insignificant and effective when they are seen in the media at all. That would be fine for approximating the ideal of ideological and political neutrality for ambassadors if it were not for the persistent assumptions and global expectations that have historically surrounded African Americans in the United Nations.

This study seeks to identify those assumptions and expectations and to see if they significantly affect or have affected African Americans in senior positions in the UN in the execution, interpretation, or evaluation of their responsibilities. The examination focuses on the role of the ambassador but the research begins with a focus on Ralph Bunche whose role as a "first" and whose breadth of responsibilities in the UN's foundation helps to define the perimeters within which race is likely to play in distinguishing between insignificance and prominence. Building on continuing issues exposed by Bunche's experience, the experiences of the three African American US ambassadors to the UN, Andrew Young, Donald McHenry, and Susan Rice, can each be examined on the basis of similar issues.

The United Nations is composed of blocks of disunited nations separated by histories of cultural and economic inequality and held together in blocks by common histories, overlapping cultures and shared economic interests. The whole is held together by a shared political and military necessity which is linked to the history of unequal political and military forces that continues to divide them. In the post WWII years since its founding, the place of U.S. diplomacy has been relatively consistent. U.S. relations with and among the UN member nations and their occasionally disruptive extra-national constituents have changed significantly while the influence of race in modifying diplomatic exchanges has ebbed and flowed. From its initial colonial and Eurocentric emergence to the post 1950s flood of newly independent states international alliances were unmade and remade generating recurrent pressures on the UN for recognition, resources, and occasionally military involvement. In the post–Cold War climate, unstable religious group accommodations and changing economic and military alliances have pushed race from the forefront of international conflict while linking it to other components of instability.

Racial Factors: National and International Pressures

Given the fundamentally representative functions of ambassadors, coupled with the policy articulation functions of diplomats generally, the emergence of race as a factor in the interactions of any UN diplomat is problematic. When any individual takes a prominent place in public, media, or policy discussions, it is very rare for the individual's race to draw particular attention and yet is just as rare for the individual's race to go unnoticed in public situations. The current concern is to determine the extent to which such notice may reach a level of political significance versus indifference. In the historically race-sensitive context such as that of U.S. national politics or in the foreign policy context of European or African relations, race conscious behavior has the potential to impose pressures that influence or deform decision-making. While it may well be politically appealing, the untested assumption that race is inconsequential flows more readily from national ideological prerogatives than from careful analysis.

Historically these pressures have been of four types:

> Internal pressure within the foreign policy or political base: (1) Positive pressures (recently more common) and (2) Negative pressures (uncommon in recent years); External pressure from domestic political opponents or foreign allies: (3) Positive pressures with high (progressive) expectations and (4) Negative pressure linked to international lobbying.

Internal pressures (A) consist of domestic demands or influence coming from inside the representative's support base, normally the Black community, based on the representative's prior interests or commitments, or they may come from the state department's own hierarchy or informal political structures. They could be either positive (A1) or negative (A2) but in modern conditions they are very unlikely to be negative. A negative pressure would involve an expectation of race-related failure making it very unlikely that the individual would have ever been selected for a position as representative in the first place. Whereas, positive pressures would imply that the ambassador's race relations would help to transcend existing cultural or racial prejudices in relations among states or cultural groups. Much as apparent ethnic or cultural links of ambassadors in the past have sometimes been thought to increase access to foreign political leaders or facilitate communications across formal barriers.

External political pressures (B) may emanate from political opponents of the current administration or from foreign allies and are focused on the assumed influence of race-related attitudes originating either with the representative or from political reactions to the racial issues and racial identity itself. These pressures, involving assumptions and expectations, are external to the state department and other American foreign policy authorities as well as the normal course of American diplomacy.

The positive external pressures (B1) come most often from the foreign "progressive" sources or from leaders in the African Diaspora expecting a progressive, race conscious influence on U.S. policy. They are positive only in the sense that there is an assumption or expectation that the interpretation of U.S. policy would be more favorably disposed toward the interests of the developing world or special sub-national groups than previously. The negative external pressures (B2) result from the opposite assumptions or expectations, that is, that the interpretation of U.S. policy would be less favorably disposed toward the interests of the developing world or special sub-national groups. Such pressures are most likely to come from those outside the African Diaspora but they may also come from within it particularly where the individual representative is burdened with a history of hostile relations in international circles separate from the United Nations.

The Bunche Model

At a time when racial identity was a salient factor in most domestic exchanges including any public events involving non-White Americans, it was readily assumed that race could have a perceptible influence on discussions and, occasionally, on outcomes however irrelevant race itself might have been to the issues at hand. At the same time, particularly in the 1940s, 1950s, and 1960s, international issues were rarely seen as significantly racial even where national groups were divided by race. Colonialism and instability, for example, might well have represented the issue focus of what was a substantially racially motivated disagreement between states but the issues actually debated in international organizations virtually never went beyond the state level composition of the issues.

However solid Bunche's individual credentials and experiences may have been—and they were impeccable—he apparently could not have reached the Nobel prize-winning position he earned without an exceptional confluence of circumstances both sad and serendipitous. As a political science professor and researcher on international relations, his selection from among wartime consultants to join the U.S. staff at the San Francisco conference establishing the UN created small waves in the State Department only in response to the uniqueness of the departure from the racial norm. Still, it was an impressive indication of racial openness but, at that point, there was not an investment of public authority comparable to that of ambassadorial appointment.

In the extended historical wake of the last post-war American attempt to form an inclusive multinational organization, the choice of American participants may have seemed less auspicious than the United Nation's eventual importance would suggest. The failure of President Woodrow Wilson to garner senatorial support for the League of Nations following WW I seems to have cast a shadow over the UN planning meetings in post-WWII San Francisco. There were still memories of the earlier recalcitrant Congress that could not have been stirred out of its ideologically grounded isolationism by careful planning, however effective, for any organizational unity of nations. As a consequence, the experimental character of including a Black representative in the meetings should have easily paled in significance behind the larger experimental character of the unpredictable organizational effort.

To some extent, the choice of Bunche was indirectly linked to a "positive" racial assumption stemming both from Bunche's prior selection for a war time consulting role and from his proposed initial responsibility in the UN Secretariat. In 1941, the US Coordinator of Information, later called the Office of Strategic Services (OSS), asked the Harvard University Department to recommend an "African specialist." The History Department responded citing a professor who referred to Bunche as the only "'Negro graduate student' he has known at Harvard who [was] able to compete for fellowships on equal terms with the better white students" (Urquhart, 101–102). That position was bridge, though uncertain, to his selection for his initial UN role as acting director of the Trusteeship Division dealing with current and former colonies. OSS perhaps heeded Bunche's own advice when he cautioned in 1942 that "the elite African especially is even more sensitive on racial matters than is the American Negro" (Urquhart, 103).

In the intervening years his experience as an advisor in the Washington-based State Department may have served as much to propel him toward the UN as to include him as American representative. He complained that the segregated environment of Washington, into which the State Department comfortably fell, left him no reason to expect that he would rise to the kind of position of responsibility that the initial UN appointment entailed (Urquhart, 133–34). Still, he was posted on loan from the State Department to the UN which indirectly made him a U.S. representative. More precisely, the appointment exposed the early positive and negative racial assumptions related to UN representation. Rather than a preference or professional choice, only the work on UN involvement in with colonial relations was initially open to Bunche. His success in developing the trusteeship program and particularly in formulating an unarmed role for UN peacekeepers opened his path to broader responsibility. In seeking to intercede in unstable colonial situations with UN pressure and occasionally with UN troops, Bunche demonstrated an agreeable and accommodating personality; one that was tolerant of diverse and even hostile political attitudes. As a consequence, the initial Africa-oriented pressures on his options exposed his potential for and value in the tense Middle Eastern negotiations.

Perhaps the first point at which an agreeable personality was essential was in working for the head of the UN negotiating team, Count Folke Bernadotte of Sweden, whose aristocratic trappings seemed excessive to many including Bunche. Although they worked together closely, both the Israeli and the Arab negotiating parties were apparently distrustful of Bernadotte. Bunche, on the other hand, was assumed to be more objective in part because he was not Swedish or European; a neutrality apparently reinforced by the fact that he was African American. Although ambiguity is arguably an external positive aspect of racial pressure, and it could be viewed as falling outside of informal Euro-American intrigues.

By the same token, such relationships would also imply negative racial pressures on other occasions. Ironically, one such occasion emerges many years later according to Bunche's own account of his awkward discussions with Congolese leaders during the chaotic and violent period of Belgian's decolonization (Henry 1999). Patrice Lumumba, in the heat of his revolutionary struggle, apparently placed little confidence in Bunche's warnings about the limits of UN support potential. At the same time, according to the then UN representative from the Congo, Thomas Kanza, "the Belgians saw Bunche 'as just another colored man. His position was very delicate in that he could never take any position or express any view about the relations between the white colonizers and the black colonized without being misinterpreted and suspected by either or both'" (Kanza1979; Urquhart 1993, 312).

In essence, the shadow of race hangs, however delicately, over the struggles and ac- complishments of Bunche's work in the UN. The significance of that influence can be usefully tested by considering the extent to which race shadows the work of subsequent African Americans carrying out representative functions in the UN. The first and most prominent issue for him, the Israeli-Palestinian conflict, suggests positive and negative racial assumptions. The second major issue, Congolese instability, though persistent, does not have the UN significance of the first. The UN's initial concern and Bunche's personal one for decolonization falls into the category of human rights which constitutes a second issue area of continuing concern to the UN.

Decolonization's significance for multi-level state conflict as well as conflict prevention exhibits two issue areas of continuous concern for the UN. In fact, Bunche's multi-state agreements for the trusteeship programs that he introduced were also the UN's introduc- tion to the building of effective alliances among states with competing economic and territorial interests. This third issue area is historically tied to the fourth continuing issue area, that of "conflict prevention." In the end and at the apex of Bunche's career, that issue may have been the most controversial and yet the least encumbered by racial fac- tors. In his 1950 Nobel Peace Prize address when Bunche warned that those who call for "preventive war" will inevitably be responsible for inciting war, he brought into focus an issue that has marked U.S. disagreements with UN members typically in the developing world through the last "coalition of the willing" in Iraq (Bunche 1950; Henry 1995).

Of four continuing issue areas—(a) the Israeli-Palestinian conflict, (b) human rights and failed states, (c) multi-state agreements, and (d) conflict prevention—only conflict prevention appears to have been uninfluenced by race in Bunche's career. Any racial influence, however, cannot be confirmed without additional evidence. A way to explore the evidence and to determine the potential and limits of racial factors is to examine these four issue areas as they intersect with the careers of subsequent African American representatives in the UN.

Ambassador Andrew Young (1977–79)

Issue Area: Israeli-Palestinian Conflict

If the presence of race as a factor in Bunche's experiences was ever speculative or ambiguous, it was far from ambiguous in the experiences of the first official African American U.S. Representative to the UN, Ambassador Andrew Young.

President Jimmy Carter's appointment of Ambassador Young in 1976 was greeted with the kind of clamor and reaction that groundbreaking events can be expected to generate. There was celebration in liberal circles, reservation in moderate circles, and noisy dis- approval in conservative ones. In the course of his three year tenure, the hostility of his initial, politically-motivated conservative critics proved contagious across the political spectrum—a contagion eased by his own race conscious faux pas. Given the early skepti- cism about him and his exclusively domestic, civil rights based, political background, his willingness to invoke race on occasion may well have stirred the diplomatic caldron.

As a consequence, the case of "negative race pressure" is generally best illustrated by Young's tenure at the UN and events in several issue areas. Particularly striking is his unfortunate reference in 1979 to the circumstances of dissident Jews detained in the Soviet Union when they were seeking to migrate to Israel (DeRoche 2003, 102–103). He apparently sought to demonstrate an openness to broader negotiations with the Soviets on the Jewish dissidents issue by admitting to past American transgressions in the case of civil rights and anti-war protestors but he grossly miscalculated the reaction at home. He was seen as disparaging the hardships of prospective Israeli immigrants in the Soviet Union. His role and reliability in dealing with Israeli-Palestinian issues among others were immediately brought into question in the U.S. Congress and in the media.

In an interview with French newspaper *Le Matin* he casually referred to American political activists in prison by saying "We still have hundreds of people that I would categorize as political prisoners in our prisons" (DeRoche 2003, 102): In response Representative Larry McDonald (R-GA) called for Young's impeachment but the motion was defeated. McDonald had already accused Young of "subordinat[ing] American interests to those of the Third World" (Jones 1996, 6) While still in Congress, Rep. Dan Qualye (R-IN) argued that Ambassador Young should resign in to "spare the nation further embarrassment" (DeRoche 2003, 103).

This largely verbal exchange would soon be aggravated by a tangible diplomatic misstep in the same issue area from which Young's ambassadorship would not recover. Young met briefly and informally with a Palestinian Liberation Organization observer at the UN in the apartment of a Kuwaiti UN representative. Angry reaction to that presumed violation of U.S. policy of non-negotiation with the PLO compelled his resignation. While the instance itself was not race-specific, the reactions were racially focused. Civil rights groups, including the NAACP, rushed to his defense (Jones, 130). The U.S. State Department, monitoring African reaction concluded that the ouster "jeopardized" diplomatic relations (Jones, 150).

Issue Area: Human Rights and Failed States

Of course, Young had done enough to provoke his conservative antagonists in Congress from the moment of his nomination by suggesting that his political experience in race relations would positively influence his approach to international relations. Particularly, when he indicated that some of our European allies were "racists," the statements were seen as unwarranted by and inappropriate for the UN context. For example, in 1977 he referred to the British in a televised statement as "chicken" on racial matters domestic and African, in Rhodesia (Zimbabwe) and South Africa; and he called the Swedish "terrible racists" (Jones 1996, 110).

Although they were unacceptable blunders for his colleagues, and they probably had an adverse impact, these incidents are linked to what may be called positive racial assumptions. First, Congress and President Carter seem to expect a human rights and race related bonus for international relations in his selection. According to a Gallup Poll, Ambassador Young was second only to Rev. Jesse Jackson as the most admired African American at the time (Jones 1996, Preface, 5). During his confirmation hearings the senators concentrated on African affairs even though they were rarely mentioned on most such occasions. The Senators' new found concern with Africa no doubt reflected what they feared or assumed was his positive disposition toward African democratization without regard to old alliances.

Young was after all the only UN representative who had ever organized "a demonstration against US foreign policy and a demonstration at the UN at that" (Haskins 1979, 11). While none of their suspicions justified any assumption that he would do more for Africa than any other American diplomat, the positive value of the racial perspective he hoped to bring to international diplomacy is indicated by his critiques of the previous administration. In a 1977 *Playboy* interview he "accused the Russians, Henry Kissinger, Richard Nixon and Gerald Ford of racism" (Jones 1996, 111).

When it came to Africa and its multi-state agreements, racial identification seems to have to given Ambassador Young a kind of confidence to speak about Africa's goals and values that would have been provocative coming from his predecessor Ambassador Daniel Moynihan. Given Moynihan's prior publicity in speaking about African Americans and social welfare policy, that image is noteworthy. Young implied that the best interests of Africa resided in imitating the West. He added that "I frankly approach Africa in terms of U.S. self-interest" (Jones 1996, 59). Although his predecessors may have agreed, the sensitivity of the topic would have prevented them from saying so. Young, on the other hand, seems to have been asserting the privilege of racially positive perspective to justify assuming a more unreserved approach.

In fact, such an approach would be consistent with the conditions surrounding his nomination by President-elect Jimmy Carter. Young was traveling with other members of the Congressional Black Caucus in Lesotho when a reporter first relayed rumors of the possible appointment. His side trip to visit a political prisoner in Africa reinforced his concern for human rights. When he returned to the United States, Carter invited him to report on the Lesotho experience and offered him the UN position. At that time, he noted that it was important that Young "had been 'associated with Martin Luther King [and that] would help people take human rights seriously from the United States'" (DeRoche 2003, 74–75). Apparently, they both saw international human rights as an elaboration of King's civil rights focus.

Issue Area: Multi-State Agreements

However positively Ambassador Young may have viewed his place in the African Diaspora as grounds for improving the American image in the UN, his international interlocutors were much less receptive. The British were clearly dismayed by his attempts to focus on their historic links to Rhodesia and apartheid South Africa. Given his consistently American-oriented approach to Africa and negative international reaction around these southern African issues, which had already provoked global consternation, European reactions to Young went beyond simple diplomatic sensitivities to more racial ones.

Still, there was a clear substantive point to Young's approach to Africa that was also expressed in the lead roles on Africa policy that President Carter accorded Vice President Mondale. On the heels of increasing American protests, especially on college campuses, against southern Africa oppression, Ambassador Young pushed President Carter to action. Carter's decision "to maintain sanctions against Southern Rhodesia in the summer of 1979 was one of the high points of Young's service in the U.N." (DeRoche 2003, 110). The fact that this decision as a broad act of foreign policy, perhaps circumventing the authority of Secretary of State Vance, is evidence of a special primacy accorded Young's perspective on Africa.

Issue Area: Conflict Prevention

While still in the confirmation process, Andrew Young sought to heighten American awareness of violent conflict in Africa as well as the potential for its spread. The Angolan civil war was seen as an immediate concern for American foreign policy. Not long after his confirmation, Ambassador Young ventured into territory unfamiliar among American diplomats by publicly affirming the potential value of Cuban military intervention as critical in minimizing African conflict. In a response during a televised Dan Rather interview he denied that Cuban troops would aggravate a "protracted guerilla war" in Angola. He added, "In fact, there's a sense in which the Cubans bring a certain stability and order" (DeRoche 2003, 76–77). He subsequently "clarified" and moderated his response but it still represented a substantial digression from the norm. Although African Americans have generally supported comparatively left-leaning foreign policy, this idea would not normally have racial overtones if it were not for his strong association with TransAfrica and its leader Randall Robinson. Among other things, TransAfrica had been an organizer of the recent trip to Lesotho. Robinson subsequently argued extensively for more open relations with Cuba to which he traveled to meet with Cuban leaders (Robinson 2000, 151–54). While Young probably would not have agreed with Robinson's later comments on Cuba, the fact that the TransAfrica leadership and other civil rights leaders were pushing for the more open approach to Cuba and Africa that Young suggested, indicates a positive race related influence. By the same token, the likely reactive pressure from the State Department on Young to disassociate from this group indicates a "negative" influence of race-related politics. In the end these latter pressures won out and Young had to be replaced.

Ambassador Donald McHenry

Almost as if to mitigate racial sensitivities, Ambassador Young was replaced by one of the few African Americans with senior status in the State Department, Ambassador Donald McHenry. As a career diplomat, he could be expected to be much more circumspect on racially sensitive issues and, in this regard, he met the most exacting expectations. At the same time, he was expected to embody the presumed positive benefits of race relations that had been expected of Young. As the *Washington Post* rather bluntly put it: "President Carter nominated Donald F. McHenry a black career diplomat as the new U.S. ambassador to the United Nations, praising him as a 'professional' who can continue the Third World relations forged by his predecessor, Andrew Young" (*Washington Post* September 1, 1979, A9).

Issue Area: Israeli-Palestinian Conflict

Still, the international reception he received in relationship to Israeli-Palestinian questions was not without negative expectations that at least in their expression reflected racial overtones as reported by *Newsweek*:

Israeli officials are privately unhappy about Donald McHenry, the U.S. ambassador to the U.N. and the man who cast the anti-Israel vote that Jimmy Carter later renounced. Israeli sources say McHenry made a poor impression on Menahem Begin and other leaders on a recent visit. Some describe McHenry as 'arrogant' in his meeting with Begin (*Newsweek* March 17, 1980, 23).

Of course, the baggage Ambassador McHenry carried from having served as Young's deputy should not be overlooked. The issues before the two ambassadors at the UN were largely unchanged along with policies of the Carter administration although the perspectives and language of their diplomacy diverged considerably. Aside from the early association of the two that, at least in the media, had negative racial overtones, the McHenry role on these Israeli-Palestinian questions was a careful balance of political and race-neutral interaction in the UN. A background of experience for all the players apparently matters.

Issue Area: Human Rights and Failed States

Where Young came to the UN with a great deal of sympathy for Africa and its development, McHenry, it may be argued, came with a lot of empathy for Africa and a personal understanding of constraints on its development. Before he took the seat of "permanent representative" to the UN, as a diplomat in the State Department, he had developed a strong interest in the conflicts of Southern Africa and particularly in Namibia. While South Africa's human rights violations were increasingly drawing international attention, Namibia's instability in the midst of its continuing colonial subjugation, was ripe for UN intervention in the spirit of democratization. Yet, on the level of personal style, the contrast between McHenry and Young could scarcely have been more striking. McHenry continued the articulation of American human rights interests which President Carter had originally encouraged through Young. Through McHenry, however, he sought and received the kind of "professional" detachment that one would expect of a career diplomat but particularly one who would "continue the Third World relations" developed by his predecessor (*Newsweek* March 17, 1980, A9). As a consequence, the role envisioned for McHenry by Washington was probably somewhere between one free of racial influence and a positive influence of race on some of these UN issues. In any event, his reserved, though effective diplomacy, indicates that his personal image and behavior on human rights issues distinguished him more from Young than from other American UN ambassadors.

Issue Area: Multi-State Agreements

Perhaps more characteristic of his special exposure to southern Africa in his State Department background than of any sensitivity to the African Diaspora, McHenry sought to impose a strong UN on the region. In 1966, he worked on a Namibia case before the International Court of Justice that involved South Africa, Southern Rhodesia, Angola, and Mozambique. Showing an unusual attentiveness to multinational perspectives, he developed a policy paper at that time on the Liberian and Ethiopian case against Southern Africa and its oversight of Namibia (C. Kennedy 1993). Apparently, McHenry saw very early the advantages of multi-state consensus building and involvement in the resolution of national and bilateral instability.

Issue Area: Conflict Prevention

Still, questions of Namibian independence and UN relations with its militant independence organization, SWAPO, rapidly led to friction over the U.S. leadership in the UN Security Council. As UN supervised elections in Namibia approached in 1980, apartheid South African became very critical of the U.S. role as represented by McHenry. After repeated South African allegations against the UN for bias toward SWAPO, the Black independence movement, Ambassador McHenry responded:

> Regarding the South African charge of UN partiality toward SWAPO, McHenry said the Security Council, which would be in charge of the elections, had never endorsed the guerilla group as the sole representatives (*Washington Post* September 10, 1980: A22).

McHenry's leadership on the Namibian question was easily attributed to his extended experience, as noted above, rather than to any personal preference or political consciousness linked to African American international pressures. Unless the parameters of race-related influences are stretched to include any strong interest in Africa, then McHenry's behavior should be seen as race-neutral. The international response, however, was laden with racially significant assumptions, as suggested by the South African accusation. The suspicion of an undercover endorsement was most likely based on assumptions about the personality or personalities of the leading country representatives since previous UN policies had been largely disengaged, if not indifferent.

Ambassador Susan Rice

Susan Rice is the first African American ambassador to the UN to be born in the period of desegregation and to mature in a period when racial barriers to mobility would finally dissolve at door of the White House. Ambassador Rice was also the first to emerge from a partisan political background and yet have acquired substantial foreign policy experience. Her road to the UN had been smoothed by her role on the Obama presidential campaign staff while her ability to contribute foreign policy advice to the campaign had been refined when she was the Assistant Secretary of State for Africa under President Clinton. As such, she was well prepared to become a "team player" at the UN. She would play a role made easier by the fact that she is the only UN ambassador to be part of her country's foreign policy cabinet (Lynch 2011). Whatever inescapable attention to race-sensitive national and international issues may have emerged, any reflection on American leadership in the UN would just as likely have fallen on the White House as on her. In this context, she is as close to the "deracialized" representative as the ideal toward which sixty plus years of UN history inclines the American presence.

Still, there are continuing signs that the ideal of representation, if in sight, may not be as free from political flaws as earlier American diplomats seemed to hope. The irony of expecting to "deracialize" a political environment charged with race-related ideological differences occasionally surfaces at critical times. The expectations or pressures come from the logical assumption that African American and African political actors will continue to make decisions based on their previous political roles. First, as an international and liberal American, there was criticism of her initiatives, or lack thereof, in East Africa as Assistant Secretary of State in the Clinton Administration in dealing with the Sudan and

Rwanda. In latter case, the assumption in media commentary seems to be that she should have done more to promote Washington intervention in Rwanda. In the case of Sudan, as one blogger among others complains after her confirmation in the UN: "Susan Rice…has overplayed her hands in setting up Omar al-Bashir for war crimes so that western corporations can seize control of Sudan's natural resources" (Phlashgordon March 20, 2009). While the policy criticism could and should apply equally to Clinton representatives in the area, the sense of disappointment with application of White House policy is striking. Additional criticisms with representatives in the African Union seemed have a similar though less strident tone.

On the domestic side, Black politics and foreign policy analyst, Professor Ronald Walters, perhaps made the starkest case for negative expectations, when in retrospect he criticized the Kerry presidential campaign in *Newsweek* for not having any Black senior staffers. It was clear nevertheless that Rice was a senior staff member of Kerry campaign (*Newsweek* 2004, 52–59). Yet, as former G.W. Bush administration UN spokesman, Richard Grenell, argues in the *Huffington Post* she was seen by others as primarily very reserved, too reserved for his tastes. He comments that she is "an absentee ambassador who is 'widely inattentive' to matters before the UN and a 'weak negotiator'" (Lynch February 4, 2010).

In some sense such a reserved posture brings her closer to the ambassadorial ideal than her predecessors but the idea of detached negotiator calls to mind the constraints of the invisible man character who could not clearly commit to any political position because ambiguous racial attitudes of others left him unsure about how and where he could fit in. Still, the criticism of her negotiation prowess may well be premature and the criticism of her "inattentiveness" seems to rest on the more marginal concerns of the UN representative, such as her failure to play a major role in the United States relief effort in Haiti from UN headquarters. In fact, her extended absences from New York at the time in order to deal with her ailing parents are easily verified. By contrast, others, such as her communications deputy, Mark Kornblau praise her for pushing through tough sanctions on North Korea (Lynch February 4, 2010).

Where the personal contributions of Ambassador Rice to the U.S. influence in the UN should be most visible, they may escape media attention because of her exceptional integration into the presidential cabinet. More than in the cases of her predecessors, her presence on the UN floor has probably been managed and mellowed by Washington-based decision-making that actively ties her to Secretary of State Clinton and to President Obama. The link to Obama may well make her appear to be less responsive to civil rights organizations and Pan African lobbies' demands because the demands on the president have often assumed shared political preference that was not present in the White House.

Similarly, the human rights community's disappointment with Secretary of State, Colin Powell, over a UN initiative on racial injustice was reflected in criticism of Obama more than the secretary or the UN representative. Powell's failure to push the Bush administration beyond its refusal to fully participate in the 2001 UN High Commissioner's conference on racism held in South Africa was rehashed in the media by similar groups criticizing the Bush administration failure to encourage such a conference (Morris 2003).

Unlike General Powell and his politically-nurtured civilian boss, George Bush, President Obama and Ambassador Rice share experiences beyond race that make the hints of personal touches harder to detect. Among other things, they were both active Democratic Party mobilizers, graduates of elite universities, took office in their forties and both had prior links to Africa. Curiously, they were both outstanding basketball players in their exclusive prep schools. Obviously then, they share personal links to diverse Black communities, but their links to the typical Black political communities are strikingly marginal. Their roots in the Democratic Party, among other mainstream groups, appear far stronger than their attachments to civil and human rights associations like TransAfrica with which Andrew Young was affiliated.

However vast the changes in the social and political environment surrounding the American role in the UN may have been since its beginning, there remains a substantial continuity in the kind of political issues confronting the American representatives. Judging from State Department-oriented websites, Ambassador Rice has dealt primarily with six major issues since assuming the position. At least four of these fit in the issue areas discussed here as shown below. They include: (1) the crisis in Israel over the Turkish-based flotilla; (2) the UN sanctions resolution on North Korea; (3) human rights and government responsibility in Sudan, and (4) international responses to Iranian nuclear development (www.turtlebay.foreignpolicy.com). The other two issues—instability in Somalia, and development and climate change-related support for Africa—are historically traceable as well but less clearly so. Ironically, these latter issues are perhaps least visible in terms of UN progress but most visible in Rice's background of career experience.

Issue Area: Israeli-Palestinian Conflict

For Ambassador Rice's African American predecessors the passage through UN debates on the Middle East was particularly foreboding. For two representatives, Young and McHenry, it was an impasse in which they were forced to confront critical political and personal challenges. For McHenry it was an immediate challenge to which his response seems to have appeased his critics. For Young it was a persistent challenge. In contrast, for Bunche it was the focus of his internationally acclaimed achievement. For Ambassador Rice it is too soon to draw a broad conclusion but some patterns are already apparent.

If there is an African American model that Ambassador Rice might emulate on the Middle East issue, it would probably be Ambassador McHenry, except that her profile is much lower than his was, in this case, bordering on invisibility. As with McHenry, however, she successfully faced an early media-sensitive policy dilemma shortly after assuming office. Following an Israeli decision to board and arrest human rights activists supporting Palestinians on a Turkish flotilla approaching Israel, Turkey demanded UN condemnation of Israel. Given the bloodshed involved that debate commanded international attention in early summer 2010. Still, the articulation of the United States in the UN was largely left to Rice's deputy, Alejandro Wolff, who negotiated with Turkey in the UN Security Council while Rice advised the president (Lynch June 2, 2010).

Still, in contrast to all the predecessors, this case demonstrates a level of progress away from the racial sensitivity indicated before. There were no expectations, negative or positive, for Rice. Her performance only elicited disappointment on the political left, in the Arab world, the Developing world and, of course, in Turkey, where there were strong hopes for a change of U.S. foreign policy and not just its UN-based articulation. By the same token, she clearly reflected Washington's position in a way was neither more provocative nor reserved than White House predispositions on the Middle East generally.

Issue Area: Human Rights and Failed States

Susan Rice may have given up her primary focus on East African instability when the Clinton Administration left the White House, but when she returned to public office along with Secretary of State Clinton, East Africa would continue to demand her attention. As noted above, Sudanese leader Al Bashir had not submitted to international justice nor had he faded from international attention. Charged with war crimes before the International Criminal Court, Al Bashir has been a continuing target of Ambassador Rice. While she clearly reflects White House policy, her history on this question gives her a head start for influence with our allies and a negative image among countries, particularly in the Arab League and African Union. The disagreement apparently focuses more on the appropriateness, or lack thereof, of international intervention rather than support for the Sudanese leader's behavior.

Here, in the criticism of Ambassador Rice, there are indications of race-related expectations gone from positive to negative. Under President Clinton the choice of the relatively inexperienced and young Susan Rice as Assistant Secretary for Africa did not fit the typical profile except, of course, it is the position at its rank most commonly held by African Americans. The selections of some African Americans for state department leadership, such as the recent choice of Johnnie Carson for Assistant Secretary for Africa, have evoked immediate public and international approval on the basis of their well established careers. For African Americans and Africans responding to the choice of Rice by Clinton, race became more salient in the absence of an established track record. In addition, American missteps on other questions of humanitarian crises in Africa helped to breed a sense of disappointment as the reverse side of unjustified expectations. The crisis in Somalia only added a sense of disapproval among some in the international community that an eight year interval would not dissipate.

On the other hand, when she assumed her latest post, she sought to bring new emphasis to American humanitarian commitment by focusing on the Millennium Development goals of one the four priorities mentioned in her confirmation hearing. Noting that "President-elect Obama has called for us to invest in our common humanity," she referred to global threats of "poverty, disease, environmental degradation, rampant criminality, extremism and violence" (Rice January 15, 2009). It was a strong statement but one that stuck to the dimensions of a team player.

Issue Area: Multi-State Agreements

For some American diplomats, particularly her deputy, Mark Kornblau, Ambassador Rice has shown outstanding skill and persistence in bringing the international community together in placing restraints on states, especially the ones the United States sees as most threatening. In particular, she is viewed as playing an effective role in pushing through a UN resolution calling for sanctions on North Korea as well as contributing to the isolation of Iran (Lynch February 4, 2010). In both cases, however, the strength of White House policy does not leave much room for the individual attribution of initiative to the U.S. representative in the UN.

On the questions involving multi-state action the accomplishments of the UN in the past two years are sufficiently ambiguous that affirmation of individual accomplishments is difficult. For example, African Union representatives have sought UN action through the General Assembly on environmental programs and climate change. Commenting on these demands, Richard Downie of the Center for Strategic and International Studies observes: "Africa has the misfortune of being the continent least responsible for global warming but the one most likely to suffer its negative consequences" (Downie 2009). On this question there is evidence of heightened expectations for Ambassador Rice but, given her relatively extensive exposure to Africa policy issues, the absence of such expectations might also be significant. Nevertheless, the inertia of the UN might well constitute the best meter, rather than the initiative of Rice, by which any such action should be measured.

Recently, the political constraints on American efforts to build multi-state agreements was illustrated through the Obama administration's decision to veto a UN Security Council resolution denouncing the extension of Israeli settlements as an impediment to peace negotiations. The announcement of a veto, clearly a presidential decision, briefly put Ambassador Rice in the center of media attention. She was cited as being sympathetic to the concerns of the other 14 member states, as she has been to UN member concerns generally. That distinguishes her and the Obama administration from the Bush administration. Deferentially, she explained that the veto should not be interpreted to mean, "we support settlement activity . . . . Continued settlement activity violates Israel's international commitments, devastates trust between the parties and threatens the prospects for peace" (*Washington Post* February 19, 2011, A13). With this statement, she fits into the Obama administration policy much as UN Representative John Bolton fit into that of George Bush in 2006 with one notable difference. Bolton took a leading and visible role in articulating the Bush administration's skeptical, if not hostile, perspective on the UN. In contrast, Rice is indistinguishable in her formulation of policy, neither progressive nor conservative. In this regard, she may truly approach the ideal suggested above of the politically invisible ambassador. Still, multi-state agreements and negotiations that avoid awkward vetoes may require individual initiative independent of the president or secretary of state.

Issue Area: Conflict Prevention

Two of the four priorities Ambassador Rice affirmed in her confirmation testimony involve conflict prevention. First, she said we would work to "improve UN peace" keeping operations which she linked to Darfur and restraints on Sudanese government practices. Second, referring to nuclear regulation in Korea and Iran she testified that she would concentrate on "preventing the spread . . . of nuclear weapons" in Iran and Korea. For her, the Sudanese issue is tied to her relatively personal political experience under President Clinton, while the Iranian and Korean nuclear issues were relatively new and yet far more central to international media attention.

Over the years, however, Darfur had garnered substantial African and African American attention. As noted above, the African Union had disagreed with the American effort she led to bring the Sudanese leader before the International Criminal Court for human rights violations. This disagreement may have led to fairly negative assumptions among African leaders about her emerging role in the UN. On the other hand, any expectations or pressures should have been counterbalanced by the heavier American pressure for sanctions intended to prevent militia or government aggression in that Sudanese region. In particular, liberal American and African American groups including TransAfrica were prominent in pushing for U.S. and UN intervention programs. The similarity of diverse American interest-group interests with that of the national government in peace-keeping has meant that the special interests of African American groups are not clearly special.

Accordingly, the U.S. representative in the UN can once again fade into the racially undifferentiated American background. It is a far cry from the period in which Andrew Young held the American UN chair but, ironically, when it comes to Africa, it is not that far from the position taken by Ralph Bunche in seeking to keep peace in the Congo, Sudan's neighborhood. When Bunche warned against individual state claims of "preventive war" in his Nobel Prize address in 1950, he was referring substantially to the Korean War. Now, over sixty years later, the UN is committed to supplanting any attempts by individual nations to militarily prevent other countries from initiating aggressive action. Ambassador Rice's affirmation of that UN role consequently looks a lot less like an individual contribution and more like standard American, liberal policy. Special interests, beyond those of defense-related associations, do not stand out, and African American interests on these issues are largely invisible. The parameters of Rice's individual initiative are therefore set by the Obama administration, to which she intricately belongs, in ways that are uncharacteristic of any previous African American representative in the UN.

Conclusion

"Ultimately," Susan Rice concludes in a Brookings Institution publication, "building effective states in the developing world . . . must become a significant component of U.S. national security policy" (Rice et al. 2010, 38). Ironically, this rather scholarly reflection on U.S. foreign policy might well have suited the first African American in the UN except for primacy given American global interests. Ralph Bunche began his UN career by encouraging peace-keeping intervention from Western countries in Africa and the Middle East while promoting national independence in the developing world. While he doubtlessly saw that change as being in the best interests of the United States and the Western world, the policy focus was on development. For Ambassador Young, who followed two decades later, the policy focus of his comments on Africa was closest to development as a means of encouraging and strengthening alliances. Young's advocacy for the developing world overshadowed other Americans for its intensity and openness but it was seemingly shared by his successor Ambassador McHenry. McHenry, though less vocal, was forceful in his insistence on the elimination of many lingering colonial constraints on African political development. Yet, it is only with the emergence of Susan Rice that the part of the world is seen primarily through the lens of American interests.

That is an unusual perspective for African American policy analysts who have generally responded to audiences influenced by African supportive lobbies and human rights groups. It is noteworthy particularly because she took this position before becoming ambassador in contrast to the more "pro-development" stances of others while in the UN. In her continuing leadership in the UN she has remained consistent with the central emphasis of her earlier position. When Ralph Bunche arrived at UN headquarters, no one knew quite what to expect except his solid professionalism; an expectation based on his background in the

State Department although national and international evidence of unrefined racism was inescapable. When Young arrived positive and negative expectations relating to African American civil rights activity and African interests were on full public display. With the arrival of McHenry the public focus, though colored by race-related expectations, largely returned to his professionalism but initially as a form of deracializing remediation of his predecessor. Finally, with the arrival of Rice, international sensitivities to her political past, working on Africa, may remain but on the national level her representation of the United States seems to bring the long sought invisibility of race to the African American international presence. Of course, the problem with such invisibility in American political history, using the images of Ralph Ellison, is that it tends to generalize to other aspects of political activity. It may now be possible for African Americans to expect to hold and leave office in the UN leaving behind only a footprint of professionalism in diplomacy rather than an imprint of their individual and ideological political impact.

References

Bunche, Ralph J. 1953. "Installation of Phi Beta Kappa, Gamma of the District of Columbia." Howard University Speech (unpublished). Washington, DC, April.

———. 1950. "Some Reflections on Peace in Our Time." *Nobel Lecture*, Oslo, Norway, December 11.

Downie, Richard. 2009. "Africa at the U.N. General Assembly," Center for Strategic and International Studies, (September 18), http://csis.org/publication/Africa-un-general-assembly.

Haskins, James. 1979. *Andrew Young: Man with a Mission*. New York: William Morrow & Co.

Henry, Charles P. 1995. *Ralph J. Bunche: Selected Speeches & Writings*, Ann Arbor, MI: University of Michigan Press.

———. 1999. *Ralph J. Bunche: Model Negro or American Other?* New York: New York University Press.

Kennedy, Charles. 1998. "Interview with Donald F. McHenry," Foreign Affairs Oral History Collection of the Association for Diplomatic Studies and Training (1993), Library of Congress.

Lynch, Colum. 2011. "U.S. Uses Veto to Block Anti-Israel Vote at U.N." *The Washington Post* (February 19).

———. 2011. "Meet the Key Players in the Iran Sanctions Debate." *Turtle Bay* (February 4 & 10): http://turtlebay.foreignpolicy.com.

Morris, Lorenzo. 2003. "Symptoms of Withdrawal-The U.N. the U.S., Racism and Reparations." *Howard Scroll: The Social Justice Law Review* 6.

———. 2006. "Ralph J. Bunche and His Intellectual Offspring." *Government & Politics* 3: Spring.

Newsweek. 2004. "Interview: Ken Rudin and Ron Walters Discuss How the Dominant Agenda May Affect the Presidential Race." (May 17): 52–59.

Rice, Susan E. 2009. "Statement of U.S. Permanent Representative-Designate to the United Nations," U.S. Senate Foreign Relations Committee, January 15.

Rice, Susan E., Corrine Graf, and Carlos Pascual. 2010. *Confronting Poverty: Weak States and U.S. National Security*, Washington, DC: The Brookings Institution.

Robinson, Randall. 2000. *The Debt: What America Owes to Blacks*. New York: Dutton.

Roeder, Bill. 1980. "Donald McHenry Irks the Israelis." *Newsweek* (March 17): 23.

Ottaway, David B. 1980. "South Africa Questioning U.N. Fairness in Namibia." *The Washington Post* (September 10).

Schram, Martin and James L. Rowe. 1979. "Young Deputy Named to Succeed Him." *The Washington Post* (September 1).

Urquhart, Brian. 1993. *Ralph Bunche: An American Life*. New York: W.W. Norton.

Shirkers and Drug Runners: The Limits of US-Bilateral Counter-Narcotics Cooperation in the Caribbean Basin

Horace A. Bartilow and Kihong Eom

American policy makers contend that drug trafficking and terrorism are inextricably linked. If terrorism is financed via the drug trade, then international collaboration to combat narco trafficking becomes a major component in the war on terror. In his testimony before the Senate Judiciary Committee on Technology, Terrorism, and Government Information, Asa Hutchinson, former Drug Enforcement Administrator, noted:

> I appear before you today to testify on the nexus between international drug trafficking and terrorism, commonly referred to as narco-terrorism. As the tragic events that occurred on September 11, 2001 so shockingly demonstrated, terrorist organizations and the dependence on and relation of some of these organizations to international drug trafficking poses a threat to the national security of the United States. Consequently, the DEA has directed enforcement and intelligence assets to identify, investigate, and dismantle all organizations, including terrorist groups, engaged in the drug trafficking trade. The degree to which terrorist organizations utilize drug profits to finance their horrific activities is of paramount concern to the DEA (United States Senate Judiciary Subcommittee, 2002)

Within the Western Hemisphere, an essential centerpiece of America's international cooperation to combat narco trafficking consists of the various bilateral drug interdiction agreements that the United States has signed with numerous countries in Central America and the Caribbean (the Caribbean Basin). The Caribbean Basin's geographic proximity to South and North America makes it a major trans-shipment center for South American cocaine that is destined for markets in the United States. The region has become a key corridor for trafficking cocaine into the United States mainly through Mexico, Jamaica, and Haiti; and to a lesser degree, through Puerto Rico, the Bahamas, and the Dominican Republic (The Strategic South American/Caribbean Unit, 2001). According to American policy makers, a major security threat to the United States is the trans-shipment of large amounts of cocaine through the region (Perl 1993–1994; Tokatlian 1994).

An important question that this article addresses is: do US bilateral drug interdiction agreements with drug transit countries, induce foreign country cooperation against drug trafficking? Does American economic aid induce foreign countries' cooperation in narcotic interdiction? These questions have captured the imagination of policy makers and scholars alike. Various answers have been provided along with suggested policy recommendations. Anecdotal evidence is typically evoked, but systematic evidence is scarce. This article seeks to fill this empirical lacuna.

In answering these questions, a simple two-player drug interdiction game is presented, which demonstrates that an essential characteristic of the incentive structure of bilateral counter-narcotic interdiction regimes is that member states of these regimes will tend to find it in their own best interest to engage in some degree of shirking. However, given the fact that North American customers are the primary targets for transnational drug smugglers, drug transit countries in the Caribbean Basin, relative to the United States, have a greater incentive to engage in shirking. We empirically test the theoretical predictions of the two-player drug interdiction game by analyzing cocaine seizure data for Caribbean Basin countries during 1984 and 2003 using a time series cross-sectional model.[1] The theoretical prediction from the game analysis found strong empirical support. Since drug trafficking is unobservable, the methodological innovation of our research design includes proxy variables that have emerged from extensive interviews with drug enforcement officials in Canada and the United States as well as throughout the Caribbean Basin and Latin America. These proxy indicators capture the incentive structure that shapes the underlying level of drug trafficking. After controlling for other confounding variables that affect the level of narco-interdiction among countries in the region, U.S. bilateral counter-narcotic interdiction agreements with Caribbean Basin governments have a negative effect on the level of cocaine seized by these governments.

Since American policy makers now believe that the war on drugs has become inextricably tied to the war on terror, as witnessed by the recent strategic measures by NATO and U.S. forces to suppress the opium trade in Afghanistan that is estimated to provide the Taliban and Al Qaeda with $100 million per year (*Drug War Chronicle* 2008), the policy implication from our analysis suggests that the existing structure of America's counter-narcotic interdiction cooperation with foreign countries needs revision to provide incentives to discourage foreign actors from shirking.

In the next section we develop the theoretical argument, which presents a simple two-player drug interdiction game that highlights the incentives to small drug transit countries to shirk bilateral drug interdiction cooperation with countries that are the primary destination market for drug smugglers. Following this discussion an empirical test of the central hypothesis derived from the two-player game is provided. Here, we proceed with a discussion of the operationalization of the primary explanatory and dependent variables in our study. We then discuss the limitations of doing empirical research using drug interdiction data and discuss how our research design addresses these problems. We discuss how the central variables of our study are operationalized and measured. We then discuss the statistical model that is used to estimate the data and conclude with a detailed discussion of the results and the implications for U.S. policy that follows from our research.

The Theoretical Argument

To answer the question of whether U.S. bilateral counter-narcotic interdiction agreements with drug transit countries induce foreign country cooperation against drug trafficking, we begin with a simple two-player narco-interdiction game. We make assumptions about the characteristics of the players, the constraints under which they make their strategic decisions and the relative payoffs each player receives as a result of the strategic choices they make. We consider two different scenarios under which players make their strategic decisions: the first, assumes that there are only two players and that drug trafficking is observable, and monitoring to discourage cheating is perfect; the second, assumes that there are more than two players and that drug trafficking is unobservable and monitoring is imperfect.

Scenario One: Observability and Perfect Monitoring

First, we assume that Big State and Little State are the *only two players* in this game. Second, we assume that both states incur costs to interdict drugs. On average, the cost of drug interdiction is higher for Big State than it is for Little State because Big State has more land, air, and seaways to patrol: PCB > PC where PCB is the patrol cost for Big State and PC is the patrol cost for Little State. Third, we make the strong assumption that drug trafficking is a phenomenon that is *observable* by both states. We also assume that security is a *public good*, since both Big and Little State benefit from it regardless of whether or not they contribute to its production. Moreover, it is assumed that drug trafficking threatens the *relative security* of both Big and Little State. Given its small market and lower per capita income, drug traffickers largely use Little State as a transit center to smuggle drugs into Big State where the prices for drugs are much higher than in Little State. A small portion of the drugs smuggled through Little State leaks out to Little State's customers, but given Big State's larger economy of scale and high per capita income, drug smugglers primarily target Big State's richer customers.

Since security is a public good, and that relative to Little State drug trafficking, represents an *asymmetrical security threat* to Big State, then Little State realizes that its individual drug interdiction efforts will have little impact on the probability that security will be produced. Instead, Little State is tempted to free ride knowing that Big State will interdict and produce security. However, since drug trafficking is observable, Big State can effectively monitor Little State's behavior at a minimal cost. Big State can, therefore, provide *economic aid* to Little State that is commensurate with Little State's interdiction effort or punish Little State for lack of effort. As a result of effective monitoring, Big State can effectively discourage Little State from free riding and maximize Little State's level of drug interdiction. We then can assume that the economic benefit accrued to Little State from cooperating with Big State is greater than Little State's patrol cost to interdict drugs: EA > PC$_L$ where EA is the economic aid Little State receives from cooperating with Big State and PC$_L$ is the patrol cost of Little State's drug interdiction. Big State's calculi for drug interdiction are as follows:

U(Big State) − f(G$_B$, C$_B$)
G$_B$ = f(SB$_B$)
C$_B$ = f(PC$_B$, MC)

Little State's calculi for drug interdiction are as follows:

U(Little State) = f(G$_L$, C$_L$)
G$_L$ = f(SB$_L$, EA)
C$_L$ = f(PC$_L$)

where U is the expected utility for both Big and Little State, f is a functional form, and G_B and G_L, respectively, represent the gains for Big State and Little State from drug interdiction. C_B and C_L, respectively, represent the cost of drug interdiction for Big State and Little State. SB_B and SB_L, respectively, represent the security benefits for Big State and Little State. PC_B and PC_L, respectively, represent the patrol cost for Big State and Little State. MC represents Big State's monitoring cost for monitoring Little State's counter-narcotic behavior. And EA is the economic aid Little State receives from Big State to encourage Little State's cooperation.

Under conditions where drug trafficking is observable and monitoring is perfect, we can easily find the Nash equilibrium: Little State interdicts but Big State shirks. Figure 1 shows the extensive form of the two-player game.

The *root node* is at the top of the tree (the little dot is labeled "Big State") and it has two branches, labeled S or s (shirk) and I or i (interdict). This means that Big State gets to choose and can go either left (S) or right (I). There are also two nodes that are labeled "Little State" and in each, Little State can shirk (s) or interdict (i). At the bottom of the game tree are four terminal nodes. At each terminal node is the payoff to the two players, Big State and Little State, if they choose the strategies that lead them to that particular terminal node. At the leftmost terminal node where both states choose (Ss), the payoff is $(-MC, 0)$. At the rightmost terminal node where both states choose (Ii), costing Big State $(PC_B - MC)$, after which Big State gains SB_B and Little State gains $(SB_L + EA)$ with costs PC_L. Their net payoffs are thus $(SB_B - PCB - MC, SB_L + EA - PC_L)$. If Big State interdicts while Little State shirks, Big State receives $(SBB - PCB - MC)$ and Little State receive (SBL). If Little State interdicts while Big State shirks, Big State receives $(SB_L - MC)$ but Little State receives $(SBL + EA - PCL)$.

Figure 1.
Perfect Monitoring and Drug Interdiction: Extensive Form

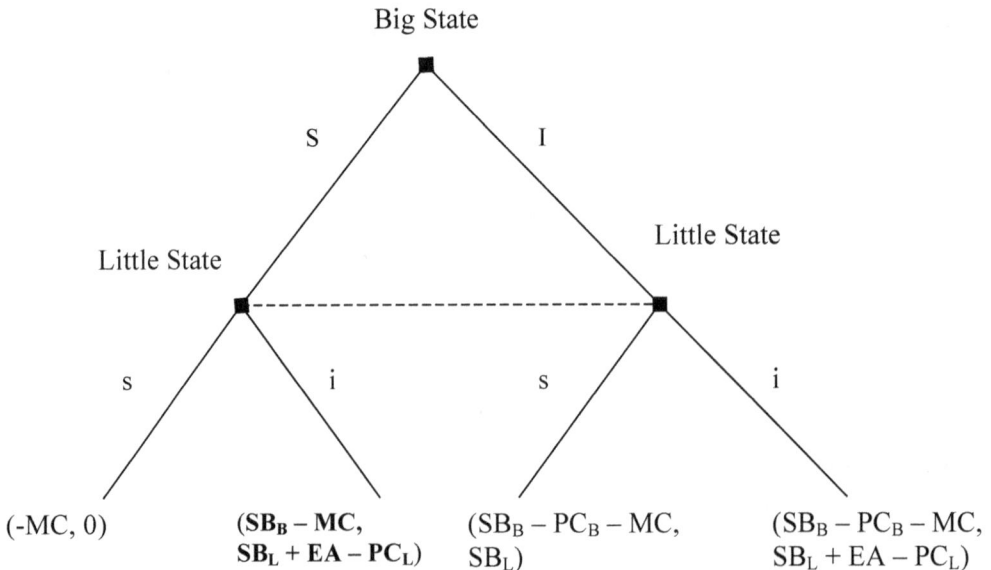

Big State

S   I

Little State   Little State

s   i   s   i

$(-MC, 0)$ $(SB_B - MC,$ $(SB_B - PC_B - MC,$ $(SB_B - PC_B - MC,$
             $SB_L + EA - PC_L)$ $SB_L)$ $SB_L + EA - PC_L)$

Figure 2.
Perfect Monitoring and Drug Interdiction: Normal Form

Little State

		i	s
Big State	I	$(SB_B - PC_B - MC, SB_L + EA - PC_L)$	$(SB_B - PC_B - MC, SB_L)$
	S	$(\textbf{SB}_B - \textbf{MC}, \textbf{SB}_L + \textbf{EA} - \textbf{PC}_L)$	$(\text{-MC}, 0)$

It is difficult to see the equilibrium point in the extensive form of the game because both states do not observe who moves first. This consideration is reflected on the dotted line connecting the two places where Little State chooses. This is called an Information Set, which is a set of nodes at which (a) the same player chooses and (b) the player choosing does not know which particular node represents the actual choice made. In the normal form of the game below, Figure 2, it is easy to see that (S, i) is the Nash equilibrium. In this simultaneous game Big State is likely to shirk while Little State is likely to interdict. This result is consistent with the arguments of David Mares who argues that U.S. policy preference has always sought to place the burden of drug interdiction on foreign countries. Essentially, he argues that rather than pay greater domestic costs at home in order to decrease drug consumption in the United States, the preference of American policy makers is to shift the burden of interdiction to foreign countries (Mares 1992).

As a result of Big State's effective monitoring and the provision of economic aid to Little State, Big State can effectively discourage Little State from shirking and maximize Little State's level of narco-interdiction. The two-player drug interdiction game, under the first scenario, generates the following proposition:

H. 1. Big State's bilateral counter-narcotic interdiction agreement with Little State will have a positive effect on the level of Little State's drug seizures.

Scenario Two: Unobservability and Imperfect Monitoring

Under this scenario we assume that drug trafficking is *unobservable* and the number of Little States who serve as transit points by traffickers to smuggle drugs into Big State has increased. Consequently, Big State monitoring of Little States has become both ineffective and more costly. As a result of the unobservability of drug trafficking, the marginal interdiction effort of each individual Little State is difficult and perhaps impossible to determine; thus in the absence of effective monitoring of each Little State's behavior, Big State cannot provide financial rewards that are commensurate with the individual drug interdiction effort of each Little State. Big State's reward to Little States must proceed according to some other rule—a flat rate of economic aid, for example, that does not depend on knowing each Little States' impact in combating the drug trade.

Figures 3 and 4 represent the changes in the assumptions under which drug trafficking takes place and the ensuing payoff functions. The changes in the payoff functions relate to Big State's increased monitoring cost and the provision of a flat rate of economic aid to

Figure 3.
Imperfect Monitoring and Drug Interdiction: Extensive Form

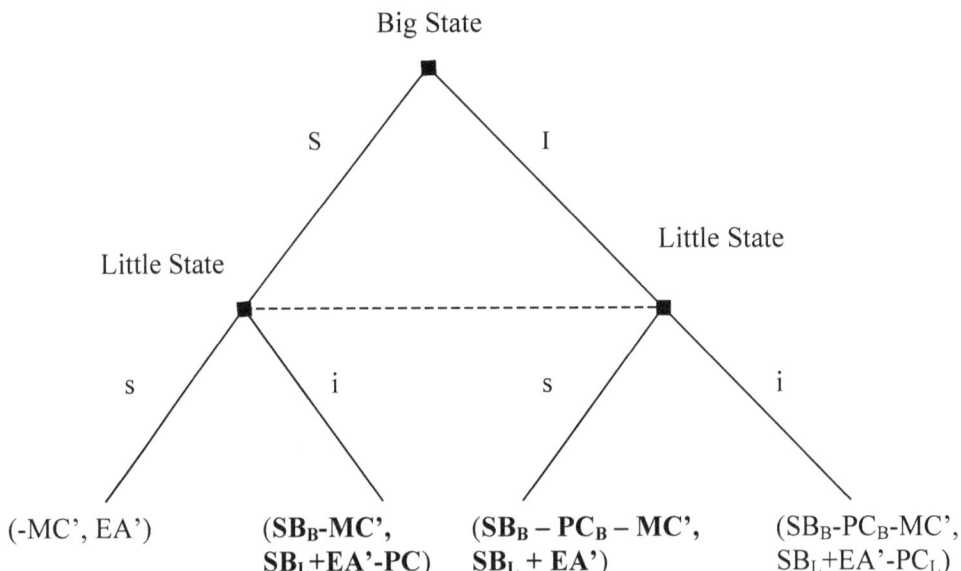

Big State

S   I

Little State   Little State

s   i   s   i

$(-MC', EA')$ **$(SB_B\text{-}MC',$**   **$(SB_B - PC_B - MC',$** $(SB_B\text{-}PC_B\text{-}MC',$
            $SB_L\text{+}EA'\text{-}PC)$ **$SB_L + EA')$** $SB_L\text{+}EA'\text{-}PC_L)$

Figure 4.
Imperfect Monitoring and Drug Interdiction: Normal Form

Little State

		i	s
Big State	I	$(SB_B\text{-}PC_B\text{-}MC', SB_L\text{+}EA'\text{-}PC_L)$	**$(SB_B - PC_B - MC', SB_L + EA')$**
	S	**$(SB_B\text{-}MC', SB_L\text{+}EA'\text{-}PC)$**	$(-MC', EA')$

Little State is regardless of the choices that Little States make: MC' > MC and EA' < EA, where MC' refers to the increasing monitoring cost for Big State and EA' refers to a flat rate of economic aid to Little States provided by Big State.

As a result of these changes in the assumptions and the subsequent payoff, while if Big State interdicts Little State will shirk (I, s). Whenever a state knows that the other state moves first or takes the initiative to interdict drugs it is tempted to shirk, because shirking reduces the cost of interdicting drug trafficking. This is a typical example of the free rider problem.

The key in this game is to know which state has the strongest incentive to interdict drugs. Which country is likely to be the major destination market for drug smugglers and tends to take the initiative to globally combat drug trafficking? We argue that the security benefits that come from drug interdiction are relatively larger for major destination countries like the United States (Big State) than they are for drug transit countries in the Caribbean Basin (Little States). Therefore, major drug-destination countries relative to drug transit countries will have a stronger incentive to take the global initiative to combat drug trafficking by collaborating with foreign governments.

Relative to the 1980s, annual cocaine consumption in the United States declined by 50 percent by the 1990s and has since stabilized (United Nations Office on Drugs and Crime 2006, 96). However, during the period of this study, "in absolute terms (U.S. cocaine consumption and) the total number of people in treatment for cocaine abuse is still by far the highest worldwide" (United Nations Office on Drugs and Crime 2000, 59). The United States remains the single largest cocaine market worldwide, accounting for more than 40 percent of all cocaine users in the world. The annual prevalence of cocaine use in the United States between ages fifteen and sixty-four is 2.8 percent of the population or 6.38 million people. The annual prevalence of cocaine use in South America (including Central America and the Caribbean) is only 0.7 percent of the population ages from fifteen to sixty-four. In the Americas, the largest opiates market is the United States with approximately 1.2 million heroin users (United Nations Office on Drugs and Crime 2006). Since the United States, in absolute terms, is the world's largest consumer of narcotics, drug trafficking poses a greater threat to its security.

In recognizing the threat that drug trafficking poses for U.S. security, American policy makers have actively sought collaboration with foreign countries to combat the drug trade (Toro 1992). By the mid 1970s, America's policy makers noted:

> No matter how hard we fight the problem of drug abuse at home we cannot make real significant progress unless we succeed in gaining cooperation from foreign governments, because many of the serious drugs of abuse originate in foreign countries. Thus, our capability to deal with supplies of drugs available in the United States depends strongly on the interest and capability of foreign governments in drug control (The Domestic Council Drug Abuse Task Force 1975, 50).

Consequently, the goal of American drug policy has been to secure the cooperation of foreign governments in combating the drug trade.

To ensure foreign country cooperation in the war on drugs, the Reagan administration increased diplomatic pressure on foreign countries and strengthened the capacity of the United States to impose the extraterritoriality of its criminal laws throughout the Western Hemisphere. As a result, the administration introduced the Anti-Drug Abuse Act of 1986 and the priority of narcotics issues was, for the first time, placed on the international agenda. The U.S. government developed a certification practice that attempts to monitor the performance of foreign country cooperation in the drug war. The Anti-Drug Abuse Act made U.S. financial assistance conditional on foreign governments' cooperation against drug trafficking (Perl 1989; United States Senate 1988).

Since the 9/11 terrorist attacks, American policy makers have rapidly expanded their international collaboration with foreign countries to combat drug trafficking and have attempted to improve their ability to monitor foreign country cooperation. For example, the Drug Enforcement Administration (DEA) has actively worked with the governments of Russia, Germany, and Romania to integrate the law enforcement networks and databases in these countries for the purpose of creating a region-wide communication and information-sharing network. By integrating the law enforcement networks and databases of foreign countries, American policy makers hope to improve the monitoring of foreign countries and intelligence gathering in combating drug trafficking in the regions surrounding Afghanistan (United States Senate Judiciary Subcommittee 2002).

The DEA has also vastly expanded its offices around the world that monitor foreign law enforcement personnel in order to foster effective cooperative relationships against drug trafficking. In 1960, the DEA had offices in only two countries and by 2003 the DEA had established offices in eighty-two countries (see Appendix, Table 2). In monitoring its foreign partners, the DEA has established sensitive investigative units (SIU) in Afghanistan, Mexico, Colombia, Ecuador, Peru, Bolivia, Brazil, Pakistan, Thailand, and the Dominican Republic. SIUs are composed of law enforcement officers from the countries' Anti-Narcotic Force. The DEA painstakingly vets foreign law enforcement officers through a stringent selection and review process that includes periodic polygraph examinations to ensure their sustained integrity in combating drug trafficking (United States Senate Judiciary Subcommittee 2002).

To facilitate cooperation with Western Hemisphere governments against drug trafficking, American policy makers have been able to secure bilateral maritime law enforcement cooperation agreements with various countries in the Caribbean Basin. With these, the coast guard from various countries in the Caribbean Basin and U.S. Coast Guard personnel conduct combined sea and helicopter searches for vessels involved in transporting illegal drugs within the territorial waters of respective Caribbean Basin countries. U.S. Coast Guard personnel also conduct training related to boarding, searching, and seizures of suspect drug trafficking vessels. These agreements permit land and sea patrols by the U.S. Coast Guard and Navy as well as maritime searches and seizures and drug arrests by U.S. law enforcement authorities within the sovereign boundaries of Central American and Caribbean countries. By the end of 2000, fifteen Caribbean and Central American countries had signed different variations of these agreements (The Strategic South American/Caribbean Unit 2001).

The above discussion demonstrates that the security benefits that come from drug interdiction are relatively larger for major drug destination countries like the United States than they are for drug transit countries in the Caribbean Basin, and that the United States has a stronger incentive to take the initiative to combat drug trafficking through cooperation with foreign governments. As a result of Big State (the United States) taking the initiative to combat the drug trade, Little States (Caribbean Basin counties) will find it in their own interest to engage in some degree of shirking. This discussion generates the following proposition:

H.2. Big State's bilateral counter-narcotic interdiction agreements with Little States will have a negative *effect on the level of Little States' drug seizures.*

Measuring the Effects of Bilateral Counter-Narcotics Agreements on Cocaine: Interdiction in the Caribbean Basin

In the sections that follow, we empirically test hypothesis 1 and 2 by estimating cocaine seizures utilizing a time-series cross-sectional analysis of the data that spans the period 1984–2003. We acknowledge David Mares' recent argument that analysis of the drug trade that is limited to the "unholy trinity" of marijuana, cocaine, and heroin maybe inadequate due to the fact that synthetic drug consumption in the United States is a growing concern (Mares 2009). However, we maintain that since American policy makers define cocaine trafficking as a major security threat because it finances the operations of major drug cartels and narco-terrorist organizations, like the FARC and ELN in Colombia, analyzing the dynamics of counter-narcotic international cooperation against cocaine trafficking is still appropriate. We now begin discussing the operationalization of the central explanatory and dependent variables of our research.

The Primary Explanatory Variable: U.S./CB Bilateral Drug Interdiction Agreement

The primary explanatory variable measures the bilateral maritime counter-narcotic interdiction agreements between the United States and the Caribbean Basin (CB) countries in our sample. This indicator is a dichotomous variable that measures whether or not CB countries, in any given year, are signatories to a maritime counter-narcotic interdiction agreement. This variable is coded 1 if a country is party to this agreement and 0 otherwise. The U.S./CB bilateral maritime counter-narcotic interdiction indicator was collected from the *Drug Enforcement Administration (DEA)*[2] and various issues of the *International Narcotics Control Strategy Report*.

The Dependent Variable: The Level of Drug Interdiction

The dependent variable is operationalized as the yearly interdiction of cocaine measured in kilograms. The cocaine interdiction data was collected from various issues of the *Organization of American States (OAS): the Inter-American Drug Abuse Control Commission (CIC AD)*.[3]

Empirical Limitations

Attempting to estimate the effect of U.S./CB bilateral maritime counter-narcotic interdiction agreement on the level of cocaine seizures in the region presents empirical limitations. Unlike licit trade, which is observable and easily measured, empirical research on illicit trade is limited by the fact that the phenomenon is unobservable and therefore cannot be measured directly (Organization for Economic Co-operation and Development. Statistics Directorate et al. 2002). We must first consider the factors that shape the behavior of drug traffickers—since the behavior of traffickers affect the state's ability to interdict cocaine trafficking. Therefore, a significant limitation of empirical counter-narcotic interdiction research is that we cannot observe how traffickers adjust their behavior in response to the interdiction measures of drug enforcement officials (Crawford et al. 1988). In other words, if drug enforcement measures in El Salvador are rigorous in the patrol of that country's territorial waters, then traffickers seeking to penetrate the American market could simply move their smuggling operations through other countries in the region where drug enforcement surveillance may be less rigorous (Adams 2002; Green 2002). In essence, empirical research on drug interdiction must address the problem of spatial correlation. This simply means that the interdiction of drugs across countries is related. We constructed a variable that is intended to capture the effects of spatial correlation on cocaine interdiction throughout the Caribbean Basin. We define this variable as the *Drug Enforcement Effort of Neighboring CB Countries* in the region.[4]

There are other empirical limitations in the attempt to estimate the effect of U.S./CB bilateral maritime counter-narcotic interdiction agreement on the level of cocaine seizures in the region. For example, we cannot observe what portion of the total amount of cocaine that is being smuggled is actually seized. High levels of cocaine seizures may reflect the reality that more rather than less cocaine is being smuggled through countries (Bagley 1989, 46–47; Stares 1996, 11). In addressing this limitation political economists, in recent years, have developed methodological techniques that utilize proxy variables that indirectly measure illicit transfers (Bartilow 2007; Bartilow and Eom 2009a; Organization for Economic Co-operation and Development, Statistics Directorate et al. 2002). Our research design draws upon the basic logic that has informed the methodology of research on illicit transfers. Our study compensates for data imperfection by controlling for a package of proxy variables that attempt to capture the incentives that shape the underlying structure of drug trafficking (Molefsky 1982). However, our research design goes beyond previous methodological designs by generating proxy variables that have emerged from extensive interviews with DEA special agents in New York and San Diego, and interviews with drug enforcement officials in Canada, Jamaica, Belize, Trinidad and Tobago, and Colombia. With the permission from the officials at the Federal Correctional Complex in Coleman, Florida, interviews were also conducted with former drug traffickers who were willing to share their insights into the structure and complexities of drug smuggling.[5] The proxy variables that were identified by our respondents include geography, per capita national income, the level of government corruption and money laundry, trade openness, and the level of individual civil liberties.

Geographic Features: Coastline and Distance

Former traffickers and the drug enforcement officials who were interviewed consistently noted that drug trafficking is as much about covering distance as it is about acquiring wealth. Given the importance of geography for drug cartels, the geographic location and physical characteristics of the CB make it conducive to drug trafficking. Interviewed respondents noted that the length of a country's coastline is an important aspect of the incentive structure that shapes the underlying level of smuggling. Drug traffickers are more likely to move cocaine through countries with longer coastlines, which reduces the chances of detection by coast guard personnel than countries with shorter coastlines, which increases likelihood of detection.[6] All things being equal, the interviewed respondents noted that longer coastlines reduce the changes for interdiction.

Respondents indicated that the geographical distance between drug transit countries in the CB and destination markets in North America is also an important aspect of the incentive structure that shapes the underlying level of cocaine trafficking. Traffickers are more likely to move cocaine through CB countries that are closer to the United States than through CB countries that are further away.[7] Relative to countries in the region that are closer to destination markets in North America, it is expected that countries that are farther away will be less exposed to cocaine trafficking. The coastline variable for the CB countries in our sample was collected from the *CIA World Fact Book 2006,* in which a country's total coastal line is measured in kilometers. The distance variable measures the geographical distance between the capitals of CB countries and the U.S. capital and land contiguity reported in miles. This variable was taken from *Direct-Line Distances, U.S. Edition* (Fitzpatrick and Modlin 1986).

CB Countries National Income Per-Capita

Former traffickers noted that the level of wealth among the countries through which they smuggle is a critical aspect of the incentive structure of cocaine trafficking.[8] Since a portion of the cocaine that is manufactured in coca producing countries in South America and smuggled through transit CB countries is often leaked to local users before reaching their primary customers in North America, richer CB countries are likely to spend more on cocaine and will be exposed to higher levels of cocaine trafficking than countries in the region that are poor. We measure a country's per-capita national income in terms of the per-capita income purchasing power parity at current international prices. This variable was collected from the *World Bank's World Development Indicators 2006.*

U.S. National Income Per-Capita

DEA and Caribbean drug enforcement respondents noted that America's wealth drives demand for cocaine and is therefore an important aspect of the underlying structure of cocaine trafficking. Drug enforcement officials agree with academic scholarship on this issue,[9] and argue that rising wealth in the United States increases the availability of disposable income to consume illicit drugs, which will affect the level of cocaine trafficking that goes through the Caribbean Basin (Bagley 1992; Rengert 1996; Toro 1992). All things being equal, the wealthier U.S. narcotic consumers become, the more CB countries will be exposed to higher levels of cocaine trafficking, which will ultimately affect the level of interdiction in the region. Since our respondents noted that the level of cocaine interdiction among CB countries is influenced by Americans' demand for the narcotic, we therefore control for U.S. per-capita income. This variable is measured in terms of the per-capita income purchasing power parity at current international prices. This variable was collected from the *World Bank's World Development Indicators 2006.*

Government Corruption and Money Laundry

DEA drug enforcement officials interviewed noted that the level of a country's government corruption is another important aspect of the incentive structure that shapes the underlying level of cocaine trafficking.[10] Government corruption can "grease the wheels" of trafficking by improving the efficiency of smuggling—enabling traffickers to smuggle cocaine in and out of countries with impunity (Galtung 2000; Kaufmann and Wei 1999; Leff 1964; Lui 1985). Traffickers are, therefore, more likely to move cocaine through countries where government corruption is embedded into the normal operations of the state and its agents, as opposed to countries where government agents and institutions are relatively clean. Since corruption undermines the integrity of the state and its officials, high levels of corruption are expected to have a negative effect on a government's ability to interdict cocaine. The corruption variable for CB countries in our sample was collected from the *Transparency International Perception Corruption Index.* Scores on the index range from 0 (which indicates a country where business transactions are entirely penetrated by government corruption) to 10 (which indicate a government that is perfectly clean).

Interviews with DEA financial investigative agents suggest that the extent to which a country's banking and financial sectors become instruments by which smugglers can conceal, move, and launder drug proceeds is an important factor that undermines[11] states' counter-narcotic interdiction capabilities. Money laundry represents the corruption of a country's financial system. While the various service providers of a country's financial sector may not know the criminal nature of the proceeds they help to move or conceal, others, however, launder proceeds with the full knowledge of the fund's illegal origin (Financial Action Taskforce on Money Laundering 2002, 19–20). Since drug traffickers value the convenience of easily laundering drug proceeds while smuggling cocaine through various countries in the region, it is argued that countries whose banking and financial sectors fail to implement internationally recognized anti-money laundry measures, as established by the Financial Action Taskforce on Money Laundering (FATF), are less likely to interdict cocaine trafficking. Because money laundry can weaken the interdiction capabilities of states, we control for this phenomenon. The data that measure whether a country is cooperating to implement international anti-money laundry measures were collected from various issues of the *FATF*. This variable is coded 1 if a country in any given year is listed by the *FATF* as failing to implement international anti-money laundry measures or 0 otherwise.[12]

Trade Openness

Canadian border enforcement officers and their U.S. counterparts noted that a country's level of trade openness is an essential incentive that shapes the underlying level of drug trafficking. They noted that traffickers are more likely to smuggle cocaine through countries where the state plays an increasingly limited role in regulating the flow of goods, services, and people that move across its borders.[13] However, recent empirical research on the effects of trade openness on cocaine interdiction in the Americas has shown that, while trade openness has a positive effect on cocaine interdiction among coca producing countries in the region, it has no statistical significant effect on the interdiction capabilities of countries in the region where cocaine is transited to North America (Bartilow and Eom 2009b). Since our interview respondents and empirical research suggest that openness to trade affects the level of interdiction we control for its effect. The trade openness variable was collected from the *World Bank's World Development Indicators 2006* and is computed as the yearly aggregate of a country's total imports and total exports divided by its GDP.

Individual Civil Liberties

The spread of economic globalization has also given rise to the spread of democratization and individual civil liberties (Drake 1998; Monshipouri 1995). Canadian and American drug enforcement agents indicated that the level of civil liberties that citizens enjoy, is an important aspect of the incentive structure that shapes the level of narco-trafficking. They note that in countries where civil liberties are relatively high, citizens are protected from arbitrary arrest and searches by the state. While these rights protect the civil liberties of citizens they also place constraints on the ability of drug enforcement officers to combat the drug trade.[14] Drug traffickers are, therefore, more likely to smuggle cocaine through countries in the region where civil liberties are relatively high as opposed to countries where individual liberties are low and the state is not constrained by the civil liberties of its citizens. High levels of civil liberties in CB countries may shield traffickers from arbitrary state power and hence may constrain the capability of law enforcement to interdict cocaine smuggling.

The measure of individual civil liberties for CB countries in our sample was collected from the *Freedom House Index of Political Rights and Civil Liberties, 1972–2003*. The scores are rescaled from 1 to 7—where 1 is the lowest score for civil liberties and 7 is the highest.

Confounding Variables

CB Countries Drug Enforcement Personnel

Researchers in sociology and criminal justice have provided theoretical and empirical reasons for considering differences in the size of law and drug enforcement agencies in combating the drug trade (Tulder 1992). In following these researchers, we considered that differences in the size of government agencies responsible for drug enforcement would affect the level of cocaine interdiction. Specifically, it is expected that countries with larger drug enforcement personnel are more likely to have higher levels of cocaine interdictions than in countries where the number of drug enforcement personnel are small.[15] The drug enforcement personnel data were adopted from various issues of *The Military Balance* (Institute for Strategic Studies 1984–2006).

The Level of U.S. Counter-Narcotic Aid

Since an important carrot of the U.S. "certification processes" is the provision of aid to countries that American policy makers deem to be cooperating with the United States in combating narco-trafficking we control for the level of U.S. aid, which is measured in terms of U.S. counter-narcotic assistance to CB countries (Bartilow and Eom 2009b). American aid may have a positive impact on the amount of cocaine that recipient countries actually interdict. However, given our theoretical model, we expect that the level of U.S. counter-narcotic aid to CB countries will not sufficiently induce their cooperation in cocaine interdiction and will therefore not have a significant impact on the level of interdiction among them. Our data on U.S. counter-narcotic aid were collected from the U.S. Agency for International Development, U.S. Overseas Loans and Grants, and is measured in constant 2007 U.S. Dollars.[16]

The Statistical Model

The theoretical model as discussed can be written as a regression equation in which the independent variables are U.S. bilateral maritime counter-narcotic interdiction agreements with CB countries (US/CB-COUNTER-NARCO-BIAGREE), the drug enforcement effort of neighboring CB countries (NEIGHBOUR-DRUG ENFORCE-MENT-EFFORT), total coast line of CB countries (CB-COASTLINE), CB countries distance from the U.S. (CB-DISTANCE), CB countries per-capita purchasing power parity

Table 1.
Caribbean Basin Cocaine Interdiction 1984–2003

Explanatory Variables	
U.S./CB Bilateral Counter-Narcotic Interdiction Agreement	–0.703***
	(0.131)
Enforcement Effort of Neighboring Countries	0.071***
	(0.027)
Total Coast Line (Km) of CB Countries	1.362***
	(0.094)
CB Countries Distance from the U.S.	0.437
	(0.320)
CB Countries per-capita purchasing power parity	–0.049
	(0.032)
U.S. per-capita purchasing power parity	0.105***
	(0.026)
CB Countries Government Corruption/Integrity	0.184***
	(0.063)
Money Laundry in CB Countries	0.063
	(0.230)
CB Countries Drug Enforcement Personnel	0.000***
	(0.000)
CB Countries Trade Openness	0.150
	(0.180)
Individual Civil Liberties in CB Countries	–0.091
	(0.082)
U.S. Counter-Narcotic Aid to CB Countries	–0.214
	(0.226)
Constant	–0.029
	(1.262)
Observations	203
R-Square	0.46

Panel Corrected Standard errors in parentheses.

* significant at 10%; ** significant at 5%; *** significant at 1%

(CB-PER-CAP-INCOME), U.S. per-capita purchasing power parity (US PER-CAP-INCOME), government corruption in CB countries (CB-GOV CORRUPTION), money laundry in CB countries (CB-MONEY-LAUNDRY), the size of the drug enforcement personnel in CB countries (CB-DRUG-ENFORCEMENT PERSONNEL), the trade openness of CB countries (CB-TRADE-OPENNESS), individual civil liberties in CB countries (CB-CIVIL-LIBERTIES), and U.S. counter-narcotic aid to CB countries (US-COUNTER-NARCO-AID). The unit of analysis in the statistical model is the nation state where the analysis of the data in each case is cocaine interdiction in a given year. The model that is estimated is as follows:

$$
\begin{aligned}
\text{COCAINEINTERDICTION}_{it} = {} & \alpha + \beta_1 \text{US/CB-COUNTER-NARCO-BIAGREE}_{it} \\
& + \beta_2 \text{NEIGHBOUR-DRUG-ENFORCEMENT-EFFORT}_{it} \\
& + \beta_3 \text{CB-COASTLINE}_{it} + \beta_4 \text{CB-DISTANCE1}_{it} \\
& + \beta_5 \text{CB-PER-CAP-INCOME}_{it} + \beta_6 \text{US-PER-CAP-INCOME}_{it} \\
& + \beta_7 \text{CB-GOV-CORRUPTION}_{it} + \beta_8 \text{CBMONEYLAUNDRY}_{it} \\
& + \beta_9 \text{CB-DRUG-ENFORCEMENT-PERSONNEL}_{it} \\
& + \beta_{10} \text{CB-TRADE-OPENNESS}_{it} + \beta_{11} \text{CB-CIVIL-LIBERTIES}_{it} \\
& + \beta_{12} \text{US-COUNTER-NARCO-AID}_{it} + e_{it}
\end{aligned}
$$

where i is country and t is year.

The estimation method is ordinary least squares (OLS) with panel corrected standard errors (PCSE) (Beck 2001; Beck and Katz 1995). The assumptions on the error term are $E(\varepsilon_{i,t}^2) = \sigma_i^2$, $E(\varepsilon_{i,t}\varepsilon_{j,t}) = \sigma_{ij}$, and $E(\varepsilon_{i,t}\varepsilon_{i,t'}) = 0$, suggesting that spatial correlation and panel hetroscedasticity remain in the variance–covariance matrix of the residuals.

The Findings

Table 1 presents the findings of our analysis of the effects U.S./CB bilateral maritime counter-narcotic interdiction agreements on cocaine interdiction among CB countries during 1984–2003 using OLS with PCSE.

The empirical analysis supports the theoretical prediction of hypothesis two. The negative coefficient for the variable U.S./CB bilateral maritime counter-narcotic agreement on cocaine interdiction is statistically significant, suggesting that increases in the number of CB countries with whom the U.S. concludes a maritime counter-narcotic agreement, has a negative effect on CB countries interdiction of cocaine. The variable *NEIGHBOUR-DRUG-ENFORCEMENT-EFFORT* that controls for the effects of spatial correlation is positive and statistically significant, suggesting that the interdiction of cocaine across CB countries is indeed related.

How well do the proxy variables perform in capturing the incentives that structure the underlying level of drug trafficking? As predicted, the positive coefficient for the variable *CB-COASTLINE* is statistically significant, suggesting that countries with longer coastlines are likely to be more exposed to trafficking, which will have a positive effect on the interdiction of cocaine. Similarly, the positive coefficient for the variable *US-PER-CAP-INCOME*, which proxies U.S. demand for narcotics, suggests that increases in U.S. per-capita income will likely increase CB countries exposure to more trafficking, which will have a positive effect on the interdiction of cocaine.

How does the level of government corruption affect the ability of CB countries to interdict cocaine trafficking? Our government corruption variable is an index that ranges from 0, which indicates a government that is completely corrupt, to 10, which indicate the highest level of government integrity. As predicted, the coefficient for the variable *CB-GOV-CORRUPTION* is positive and statistically significant, indicating that clean governments in the region have a positive effect on cocaine interdiction. The other proxy variables, namely, CB countries distance from the U.S., the per-capita purchasing power parity of CB countries, money laundry among CB countries, and the level of civil liberties in CB countries all fail to rise to the level of statistical significance. And similar to the findings of recent research on the impact of trade openness on countries interdiction of cocaine in the Americas (Bartilow and Eom 2009b), trade openness among CB countries has no statistical significant effect on cocaine interdiction.

Finally, we consider the effects of two potentially confounding variables on CB cocaine interdiction. These are the drug enforcement personnel of CB countries and U.S. counter-narcotic aid. The positive coefficient for the variable *CB-DRUG-ENFORCEMENT-PERSONNEL* is statistically significant, indicating that increases in the size of countries drug enforcement personnel has a positive effect on cocaine interdiction. However, as predicted the variable *US-COUNTER-NARCO-AID* failed to reach statistical significance, suggesting that the level of U.S. aid to CB countries is not sufficient to induce their cooperation in the interdiction of cocaine trafficking. Essentially, what this implies is that the threat of "decertification" and the consequent denial of aid to induce foreign country cooperation with U.S. anti-drug policies is becoming an increasingly weak instrument of coercion.

Conclusion

In the post-9/11 security environment, American policy makers contend that drug trafficking and terrorism are inextricably linked. If terror is financed via the drug trade, then international collaboration to combat narco-trafficking becomes a major component in the war on terror. The important question to ascertain is the extent to which U.S. bilateral counter-narcotic agreements with transit countries induce their cooperation against drug trafficking. The Nash Equilibrium solutions of our two-player drug interdiction game predicted that both the U.S. and Caribbean Basin countries would engage in some degree of shirking. However, under conditions of imperfect monitoring and the unobservability of drug trafficking, if the United States takes the initiative and seeks out bilateral counter-narcotic cooperation with countries in the Caribbean Basin, which has been the case, then these states will tend to find it in their interest to shirk. The statistical model of cocaine interdiction among Caribbean Basin countries from 1984–2003 provides some empirical support for the existence of shirking among countries in the Caribbean Basin.

A striking example of shirking is seen in the recent struggle between the United States and Jamaican government officials over the extradition of Jamaican Drug Lord Christopher "Dudus" Coke. The DEA considered Coke to be one of the world's most dangerous narcotics traffickers, and is suspected of playing a major role in supplying marijuana, cocaine, and weapons to the East Coast of the United States. Coke's organization, which is known as the "Shower Posse," operated from West Kingston, an impoverished area, which is the stronghold of the ruling Jamaica Labor Party and is represented by Prime Minister Bruce Golding. Officials in the Obama Administration contend that the Jamaican government paid the powerful law firm of Manatt, Phelps and Phillips US$400,000 to lobby the White House and other administration officials to stop the extradition request for Coke (Eggen 2010). Moreover, the Grand Jury of the Southern District Court of New York, which indicted Coke on gun and drug trafficking, charges contend that senior Jamaican government ministers had actively blocked information required by the Court that was pertinent to the prosecution of Coke (Investigative Coverage Unit 2010). In a recent report on global narcotics trafficking, the U.S. State Department noted that the government of Jamaica's "unprecedented delays, unexplained disclosure of law enforcement information to the press, and unfounded allegations questioning U.S. compliance with the Mutual Legal Assistance Treaty (MLAT) and Jamaican law raises serious questions about the government's commitment to combating transnational crime" (U.S. State Department 2010, 382).

The tendency for shirking, however, is not limited to CB countries but is a structural characteristic of international counter-narcotic cooperation. Iran, for example, has emerged as a major transit point for heroin smuggled from Afghanistan and Pakistan—destined for markets in Europe and North America. In face of U.S. and United Nations threats of additional economic sanctions against Iran for pursuing its nuclear program, Iranian officials have recently signaled that "Iran could just look the other way as Europe is flooded with Afghan heroin" (*Drug War Chronicle* 2006). Since drug trafficking is seen as inextricably linked to terror and represents a major threat to U.S. security, American policy makers should reconsider how U.S. international cooperation with foreign countries to combat narco-trafficking could be recalibrated to provide sufficient incentives to discourage foreign countries from potentially shirking the interdiction of narcotics.

Acknowledgment: The authors would like to thank officials from the Organization of American States who provided advice and shared valuable data. The lead author thanks the drug enforcement officials from the U.S. Drug Enforcement Administration (DEA), the Royal Canadian Mounted Police, the Canadian Border Services, and drug enforcement officials in Jamaica, Trinidad and Tobago and Colombia who granted interviews.

Table 2.
DEA Overseas Offices 1960–2003

1960	1961	1963	1966	1969	1970
2	3	8	10	11	19
1971	1972	1973	1974	1975	1976
26	33	36	43	45	46
1977	1979	1981	1982	1984	1986
47	48	50	56	58	59
1987	1988	1990	1992	1997	1998
62	63	66	68	70	78
1999	2000	2002	2003		
79	80	81	82		

Source: Data was extracted from "The History of the DEA, Parts 1 & 2." The data can be accessed at: http://www.justice.gov/dea/pubs/history/history_part1.pdf; http://www.justice.gov/dea/pubs/history/history_part2.pdf

Some of these officials wish to remain anonymous. Any errors in the interpretation of the findings of this research are solely the responsibility of the authors.

Appendix

The calculation for the variable *Drug Enforcement Effort of Neighboring CB Countries*

In measuring the *Drug Enforcement Effort of Neighboring CB Countries* we calculated this variable via the following formula:

$$\frac{\sum_{i=1}^{N-1}\frac{1}{\text{Distance from }j_i}*\text{Drug Enforcement Personnel}_i}{N-1}\text{ for a single country } j,$$

where N is the total number of countries, i is a neighboring country and $i{\neq}j$. Distance from j is the distance from a single country j to a neighboring country i, and drug enforcement personnel is the number of the drug enforcement personnel in a neighboring country i. The expected relationship between the average drug interdiction effort by neighboring countries i and a single country j is positive. The drug enforcement personnel data were adopted from various issues of *The Military Balance* (Institute for Strategic Studies 1984–2006) and the distance data were collected from *Direct-Line Distances, U.S. Edition* (Fitzpatrick and Modlin 1986).

Notes

1. To empirically test our argument we also considered analyzing the interdiction of other drugs. However, interdiction data for heroine and opium are sparse and data for the interdiction of synthetic drugs are unavailable. Marijuana interdiction data are available but America policy makers do not perceive marijuana trafficking as a serious threat to US security. We, therefore, analyzed countries interdiction of cocaine largely because American policy makers have designated cocaine trafficking into the United States as a significant security threat especially since a number of terrorist groups in Colombia, namely the FARC, are involved in the production and smuggling of the drug. Shirking the interdiction of cocaine trafficking would seriously undermine US security objectives. Our sample of Caribbean basin countries include Antigua and Barbuda, the Bahamas , Barbados, Belize, Costa Rica, Dominica, the Dominican Republic, El Salvador, Grenada, Guatemala, Guyana, Haiti, Honduras, Jamaica, Nicaragua, Mexico, Panama, St. Kitts and Nevis, St. Lucia, St. Vincent and the Grenadines, Suriname, and Trinidad and Tobago. Drug interdiction data are available up to 2003.
2. DEA data can be accessed at http://www.usdoj.gov/dea/pubs/intel/01019/usvi#usvi.
3. The OAS data are available at http://www.cicad.oas.org/oid/Estadisticas/default.htm.
4. The formula that generated this variable is located in the appendix.
5. The lead author conducted interviews with DEA financial investigative agents in New York in June 2001 and with the DEA's Supervisory Special Agent of the San Diego Field Division in June 2004. This author also conducted interviews with former drug traffickers in the Federal Correctional Complex in Coleman, Florida in August 2002. Research and sabbatical grant provided travel support for interviews conducted with Drug Enforcement officials in Colombia in November 2002. Grant also provided travel support for interviews conducted with the Coast Guard and Drug Enforcement officials in Jamaica and Belize during May and June 2003. Additional financial support from the Canadian Studies Grant competition provided travel support for interviews conducted with the Drug Enforcement officers of the Canadian Royal Mounted Police and Border Service Agency in June 2006.
6. Lead author's interview with "Johnny" [pseudonym], former drug trafficker, Federal Correctional Complex, Coleman, Florida, August 14, 2002. Lead author's interview with the Jamaica Defense Force (JDF) Coast Guard personnel, June 17, 2003. Lead author's interviews with the personnel attached to the Maritime Wing of the Belize Defense Force, May 27, 2003.

7. Lead author's interview with "Green" [pseudonym], former drug trafficker, Federal Correctional Complex, Coleman, Florida, August 14, 2002. Lead author's interview with Trinidad and Tobago's Commissioner of Police and the Director of the Police Force Drug Branch, February 9, 2006.
8. Lead author's interview with "Johnny" [pseudonym], former drug trafficker, Federal Correctional Complex, Coleman, Florida, August 14, 2002. Lead author's interview with "Green" [pseudonym], former drug trafficker, Federal Correctional Complex, Coleman, Florida, August 14, 2002.
9. Lead author's interview with the DEA's Supervisory Special Agent of the San Diego Field Division, June 17, 2004 and interview with Trinidad and Tobago's Commissioner of Police and the Director of the Drug Branch, February 9, 2006.
10. Lead author's interview with the DEA's financial investigative agents in New York, June 11, 2000; DEA's Supervisory Special Agent of the San Diego Field Division in San Diego, June 17, 2004.
11. Lead author's interview with the DEA's financial investigative agents in New York, June 11, 2000.
12. Every year the FATF produces a list of countries that are not cooperating with its recommendations for implementing anti-money laundering measures. Most of the FATF recommendations relates to anti-money laundry measures that protect a country's banking sector—the traditional means by which money has been laundered. However, as we have discussed earlier, money laundering in recent years is no longer limited to the use of banks, but include a wide array of techniques that include but not limited to the securities sector, and various internet banking and gambling services, the entertainment and the travel industry, real estate, and the gold and diamond industries to name just a few. And because money-laundering techniques that exploit these varied venues are difficult to detect and monitor, we recognize that our measure is at best conservative. We also used the US State Department's *International Narcotics Strategy Report* (INCSR) classification scheme on countries whose financial systems are highly vulnerable to money laundering. Our results are robust to the use of the INC SR money laundry classification scheme. These results are available upon requests from the authors.
13. Lead author's interviews with field Directors of the US/Canadian Integrated Border Enforcement Teams (IBET's) in Ottawa, June 19, 2006.
14. In this study we adopt the definition of drug enforcement personnel as defined and identified by the U.S. State Department, the U.S. Drug enforcement Administration (DEA), and the London-Based Institute of Strategic Studies which collects this information and reports it in the publication, *The Military Balance*. Specifically, a country's drug enforcement personnel include a country's coast guard, customs agents, border police, special drug enforcement agents that are attached to a country's police force and special paramilitary drug enforcement strike forces that are attached to a country's military, navy, and air force.
15. The lead author conducted interviews with DEA special Agents in New York, and San Diego in June 11, 2001 and July 15 2004 respectively. Interviews were also conducted with drug enforcement agents attached to the Royal Canadian Mounted Police, Drug Branch, Ottowa, June 8, 2004.
16. USAID data are available at http://qesdb.cdie.org/gbk/index.html.

References

Adams, [pseudonym] Johnny. Author interview. Coleman, August 14, 2002.

Bagley, Bruce M. 1989. "The New Hundred Years War? U.S. National Security and the War on Drugs in Latin America." In *The Latin American Narcotics Trade and U.S. National Security*, edited by Donald J Mabry, 44–58. New York: Greenwood Press.

———. 1992. "Myths of Militarization: Enlisting Armed Forces in the War on Drugs." In *Drug Policy in the Americas*, edited by Peter H. Smith, 129–50. Boulder, CO: Westview.

Bartilow, Horace. 2007. "Does Drug Enforcement Reduce Crime? An Empirical Analysis of the Drug War in Central America and Caribbean Countries." In *Crime, Delinquency and Justice: A Caribbean Reader*, edited by R. Deosaran, 555–77. Kingston: Ian Randle Publishers.

Bartilow, Horace and Kihong Eom. 2009a. "Busting Drugs While Paying with Crime: The Collateral Damage of U.S. Drug Enforcement in Foreign Countries." *Foreign Policy Analysis* 5: 1–12.

———. 2009b. "Free Traders and Drug Smugglers: Does Trade Openness Weaken or Strengthen States' Ability to Combat Drug Trafficking?" *Latin American Politics and Society* 51: 117–45.

Beck, Nathaniel. 2001. "Time-Series-Cross-Section Data: What Have We Learned in the Past Few Years?" *Annual Review of Political Science* 4: 271–93.

Beck, Nathaniel and Jonathan Katz. 1995. "What to Do (and Not to Do) with Time-Series Cross-Section Data." *American Political Science Review* 89: 634–47.

Crawford, G. B., Peter Reuter, K. Isaacson, and P. Murphy. 1988. *Simulation of Adaptive Response: A Model of Drug Interdiction*. Santa Monica, CA: Rand Corporation.

Drake, Paul W. 1998. "The International Causes of Democratization." In *The Origins of Liberty: Political and Economic Liberalization in the Modern World*, edited by Paul W. Drake and Mathew D. McCubbins, 70–91. Princeton, NJ: Princeton University Press.

Drug War Chronicle. 2008. NATO, US Deepen Anti-Drug Operations in Afghanistan in Bid to Throttle Taliban. Drug War Chronicle.

———. 2006. Southwest Asia: Iran Official Says Country Could Ignore Drug Traffickers If U.N Doesn't up Anti-Drug Aid. Drug War Chronicle.

Eggen, Dan. 2010. U.S. Jamaica Relations Tested by Lobbying Dispute. *The Washington Post* (April 16).

Financial Action Taskforce on Money Laundering. 2002. Report on Money Laundering Typologies, 2001–2002. Paris: FATF Secretariat, OECD: Financial Action Task Force on Money Laundering.

Fitzpatrick, Gary L. and Marilyn J. Modlin. 1986. *Direct-Line Distances, U.S Edition*. Metuchen, NJ and London: The Scarecrow Press, Inc.

Galtung, Fredrick. 2000. "A Global Network to Curb Corruption: The Experience of Transparency International." In *The Third Force: The Rise of Transnational Civil Society*, edited by Ann M. Florini, 17–47. Washington DC: Carnegie Endowment for International Peace.

Gary L. Fitzpatrick and Marilyn J. Modlin. 1986. *Direct-Line Distances, U.S Edition*. Metuchen, NJ and London: The Scarecrow Press, Inc.

Green, [pseudonym] Jeff. Author's interview. Coleman, August 14, 2002.

Institute for Strategic Studies. 1984–2006. *The Military Balance*. London: International Institute for Strategic Studies.

Investigative Coverage Unit. 2010. "Us Government Probing Three Govt Ministers: Dudus Grand Jury Says Officials Blocking Information." *Jamaica Observer* (April 5).

Kaufmann, Daniel and Shang-Jin Wei. 1999. Does "Grease Money" Speed up the Wheels of Commerce? 1–18. Cambridge, MA: Working Paper 7093. National Bureau of Economic Research.

Leff, Nathaniel H. 1964. "Economic Development through Bureaucratic Corruption." *The American Behavioral Scientist* 8: 8–14.

Lui, Francis. 1985. "An Equilibrium Queuing Model of Bribery." *Journal of Political Economy* 93: 760–81.

Mares, David R. 2009. "Institutions, the Illegal Drug Trade and Participant Strategies: What Corrupt or Pariah States Have in Common with Liberal Democracy and the Rule of Law." *International Interactions* 3, no. 5: 207–39.

———. 1992. "The Logic of Inter-American Cooperation on Drugs." In *Drug Policy in the Americas*, edited by Peter Smith, 329–42. Boulder, CO: Westview Press.

Molefsky, Barry. 1982. "America's Underground Economy." In *The Underground Economy in the United States and Abroad*, edited by Vito Tanzi, 47–67. Toronto: Lexington Books.

Monshipouri, Mahmood. 1995. *Democratization, Liberalization & Human Rights in the Third World*. Boulder, CO: Lynne Rienner.

Organization for Economic Co-operation and Development, Statistics Directorate, International Monetary Fund, Bureau of Statistics, International Labor Organization, Bureau of Statistics, and Commonwealth of Independent States, Statistical Committee. 2002. *Measuring the Non-Observed Economy: A Handbook*. Paris: OECD.

Perl, Raphael F. 1989. "International Narcopolicy and the Role of the U.S. Congress." In *The Latin American Narcotics Trade and U.S. National Security*, edited by Donald J. Mabry, 89–102. New York: Greenwood Press.

———. 1993–1994. "Clinton's Foreign Drug Policy." *Journal of InterAmerican Studies and World Affairs* 35: 143–51.

Rengert, F. George. 1996. *The Geography of Illegal Drugs*. Boulder, CO: Westview Press.

Stares, Paul. 1996. *Global Habit: The Drug Problem in a Borderless World*. Washington, DC: Brookings Institution.

The Domestic Council Drug Abuse Task Force. 1975. White Paper on Drug Abuse, 50. Washington, DC: US Government Printing Office.

The Strategic South American/Caribbean Unit. 2001. The Drug Trade in the Caribbean: A Threat Assessment, 69: Drug Enforcement Administration.

Tokatlian, Juan G. 1994. "The Miami Summit and Drugs: A Placid, Innocuous Conference?" *Journal of InterAmerican Studies and World Affairs* 36: 77–82.

Toro, Maria Celia. 1992. "Unilateralism and Bilateralism." In *Drug Policy in the Americas*, edited by Peter H. Smith, 314–28. Boulder, CO: Westview Press.

Tulder, Frank van. 1992. Crime, Detection Rate, and the Police: A Macro Approach. *Journal of Quantitative Criminology* 8: 113–31.

U.S. State Department. 2010. *2010: International Narcotic Control Strategy Report*. Washington DC: State Department.

United Nations Office on Drugs and Crime. 2000. *World Drug Report 2000*. Geneva: United Nations.

———. 2006. *2006: World Drug Report*. Geneva: United Nations.

United States Senate. 1988. International Narcotics Control and Foreign Affairs Certification: Requirements, Procedures, Timetables, and Guidelines. 100 Cong., 2d Sess, March. Washington DC.

United States Senate Judiciary Subcommittee. 2002. International Drug Trafficking and Terrorism, 1–6. Washington, DC: The Senate Judiciary Committee Subcommittee on Technology, Terrorism, and Government Information.

Works in Progress

The Fragmented Rainbow Project

Michael C. Dawson*

My research career took a strange turn over the past decade. What was supposed to be a concise and contained book project based on public opinion data from the 2000 presidential elections turned into a decade long project that evolved to include eight separate public opinion studies between 2000 and 2010, three separate book projects, and a research paper to be submitted to a journal. There were major missteps along the way, and far too much time between publication of *Black Visions* (University of Chicago Press 2001) and the first of the three books (*Not in Our Lifetimes*, University of Chicago Press 2011). There were side projects that diverted time from the main project. All in all, I was involved in a research process that any tenured colleague, including most definitely myself, would stridently tell our junior colleagues to avoid if they wanted to see their careers progress—and we would be absolutely right to give them that advice.

Yet, this curious process, one which I fervently hope I will never be involved in again, yielded a unique (for me) opportunity to be able to pursue a range of questions across methodologies and audiences that would have been difficult with a more conventional approach. First, I was able to write three books, all being published (hopefully) within 18–24 months of each other, that address critical problems within Black politics.

The first of these manuscripts is *Not in Our Lifetimes: The Future of Black Politics* (The University of Chicago Press, 2011). In this, I argue that Black politics had reached a nadir by 2005. Rebuilding a robust Black politics is made even more difficult, I argue, as Black elites in all domains of activity, and large segments of the Black middle class have embraced the anti-politics of neoliberalism. Public opinion data are used to probe both the problems facing Black politics, and more generally the political consequences of the massive racial divide in contemporary American politics. This book is aimed at a trade audience, and explicitly espouses a political position.

The second of these manuscripts, *Blacks In and Out of the Left: Past Present and Future,* is currently under review and should be out sometime during 2012. This book, based on my 2009 Du Bois lectures at Harvard University, *examines* the two most active phases of twentieth century of Black leftist insurgency: 1917–1940 (53) and 1964–1980. The key question going forward for Black politics, and specifically radical Black politics is, "what is to be done" or "where do we go from here" as Martin Luther King framed the same question in 1967. There are important lessons from both periods, I argue, for rebuilding a progressive Black politics. I also critique various theorists' narratives of the Black Power Movement that claim that Black movements and their "imitators" (according to critics such as Todd Gitlin) were responsible for the fragmentation of the left, and more generally, progressive politics in the latter third of the twentieth century.

The final book manuscript is *Reflections on Black Politics in the Early 21st Century* 2012. This manuscript is currently being completed and will be submitted at the beginning of 2012 for review. *Reflections* concentrates on the statistical analysis of the determinants of racial attitudes and the massive changes in racial attitudes, particularly among Blacks and Latinos (the groups with the largest changes), that occurred between 2008 and 2010. *Reflections* also more explicitly engages the political theory literature using that literature to engage such questions as what traditional, if any, modes of Black political leadership are relevant for contemporary Black politics. This book is the most traditional political science manuscript of the three (to the degree that any of my work can be loosely labeled "traditional political science").

There are common themes that loosely tie all three manuscripts to each other and which motivated the research of the Fragmented Rainbow Project. I take the position in all three manuscripts that in the United States there is a hierarchical social structure based on racial subordination—the racial order—that still shapes American politics, discourse, civil society, and economic and political institutions to the disadvantage of all non-White populations. It is a *dangerous fallacy* to believe the United States has become a post-racial society despite the statements (and desires) of some liberal and many conservative commentators. The racial order has evolved rapidly, particularly with the 1965 passage of more expansive immigration laws that greatly accelerated immigration from Latin America and Asia. While the often deadly cleavage between Blacks and Whites never defined the racial terrain as decisively as commonly conceived, it is now questionable, some argue, whether the Black/White divide remains the critical structural feature of the racial order. Empirically, I address this question by showing how the racial order, at least as reflected in American public opinion, is complicated, but suggest that generally, if not rigidly, Blacks and Whites still usually anchor the opposite ends of the public opinion spectrum.

I further argue that Black politics remains weaker than it has been for generations and must be rebuilt for Blacks to continue their quest for racial justice and equality within the new racial order. One obstacle to rebuilding Black politics has been that neoliberalism has taken hold among Black elites and the Black middle class, and as a consequence, the Black disciples of neoliberalism have embraced an extremely narrow definition of politics. All three books in different ways aim to engage debates within Black politics, progressive politics, and the study of race and politics.

My work on this project started with a concentration on how the intersection of race and class was now affecting Black and more generally American politics—a theme I had not addressed in depth since the publication of *Behind the Mule*. The project expanded to also include themes of intersectionality first developed within Black feminist theory, and attempts to use these themes to theorize the different dimensions of the racial order within the United States. That is to say the project explores intersectionality from perspective of the intersection of race across different structural orders such as those of class and patriarchy.

As the last paragraph suggests, the Fragmented Rainbow Project has eclectic theoretical foundations. Critical race theory, democratic theory, feminist theory, continental political theory, and African American political thought are some of the more important theoretical literatures that are used as resources. The empirical research uses primarily quantitative methodology, but that is the nature for better *and* worse of most empirical work in public opinion. Of course, I also use interpretive methodologies in analyzing politics, the quantitative research findings, and for the interpretation of history, as well as broader theorizing.

As stated, the project was designed to address multiple audiences. These audiences include a general lay audience (particularly those interested in race, Black Studies, and progressive politics); undergraduate and graduate students; and for the more technical work, colleagues in political and allied social sciences. One of the advantages of having a multi-manuscript research project is the ability to be able to attempt to reach different audiences more precisely, and to tackle common questions from different angles.

My work has always been synthetic in the sense that I draw on work across subdisciplines and the disciplines more generally ranging from computer science to literary theory. While my empirical work has often used quantitative methods found within the mainstream of political science, the subject of that empirical work, the theorizing that I attempt, and the implicit and explicit political connotations of my work put a good deal of my work including two out of the three (or probably all three) of my current book manuscripts outside of the mainstream of political science, and certainly my putative subfield of American politics.

The most important reason that I am grateful that I had the opportunity to work through this strange and often frustrating project is that I have been afforded an opportunity that is too often denied political scientists. I have been able to the best of my ability use research on Black politics to hopefully influence the discourse in *and* outside of the academy on the future of race and politics within the United States.

Note

*   Michael C. Dawson is the John D. MacArthur Professor of Political Science and Director of the Center for the Study of Race Politics & Culture, The University of Chicago.

My Research Approach

Andra Gillespie*

Journalism schools teach reporters to answer the five W's (and one H)—who, what, when, where, why, and how—in each story they write. As political scientists, we should think about half of this list whenever we pick a new research topic. We need to be clear about what we study, how we study it, and why we study it in the first place. So, in this essay, I'd like to use the framework of two W's (and one H) to flesh out the what, how, and why of my research. As I do this, I provide general tips that any scholar can apply to his or her work.

What I Do

I took a somewhat circuitous route to my current research agenda. For my dissertation, I studied the effect of canvassing on Black voter turnout using field experiments. It was a fine research topic, but at the end of the day, it did not fully capture my imagination. Fortunately, my field experimental work took me to Newark, New Jersey, where I had the good fortune to witness the 2002 mayoral contest between Cory Booker and Sharpe James. While I collected important data on turnout during that election, I found myself asking a new set of questions about generational transition in Black politics. Was the acrimony between old and young leaders a matter of style or substance? Why were the younger leaders so appealing to some voters and repulsive to others? Will the younger leaders be in a better position to improve the material conditions of Blacks than their elders? The questions that I started asking after 2002 continue to shape my research agenda today.

I continued to do work on voter turnout, but gradually, it became clear that I should pursue research in Black leadership studies. Along the way, I received feedback that helped to shape my agenda. For instance, after presenting a paper on the 2002 Newark mayoral race in a departmental colloquium at Emory, my colleagues pushed me to put my observations about Newark into a national context. That feedback, coupled with support I received at NCOBPS, led to the publication of my edited volume, *Whose Black Politics? Cases in Post-Racial Black Leadership* (Gillespie 2010).

My journey has taught me a number of things about crafting a research agenda. First, observation has been critical to my developing research questions. Most scholars learn quickly that mastering the political science literature is the first step toward developing good research questions. In many instances, though, the second step may involve real-world observation. For me, watching two Black Democrats fight a "blacker than thou" campaign for political office generated a whole new set of ideas which drove me back to the literature to develop testable questions.

The biggest lesson that I have learned about crafting a research agenda is that each and every scholar should own her agenda. Often, young scholars feel pressure to study what their advisors want them to study or what is popular at any given moment. Those who succumb to that pressure, though, will probably be miserable, and the quality of their work will suffer. Keep in mind that most scholars usually stick with a line of research for a decade or more, publishing numerous articles and books before they truly pick up another topic. If one is not enthused about a topic at the beginning of a project, I guarantee that she will probably hate it by the end of the project.

There are some caveats to this advice. First, I cannot promise that passion for a certain research subject will guarantee tenure or twenty peer-reviewed publications. One has to judge for herself if she is willing to take the risks needed to take ownership of her research agenda (Incidentally, timing considerations will compel advanced assistant professors to wait to change topics until they have finished publishing from their initial project). It should also be noted that owning one's research agenda does not free one from the constraints of what counts for acceptable research in our discipline (i.e., publishing in highly regarded peer reviewed journals, etc.).

Second, it must be noted that some people are passionate about dead-end research subjects. They need to be open to constructive criticism on this matter, and discerning about the spirit in which such critiques are levied.

In general, though, if a scholar is asking relevant questions and framing them as testable hypotheses, she should feel comfortable shaping her research agenda as she sees fit.

How I Do It

For me, question generation directly relates to issues of methodological choice. I agree with King et al. (1994) that all political science should be systematic, regardless of method. Moreover, my graduate school professors emphasized the importance of question-driven research. They taught me to come up with good questions first, then find the appropriate data and methods to answer those questions. It is a simple concept, but given the methodological polarization that pervades our discipline, it is clear that we must constantly remind ourselves of this principle.

In my own work, I tend to employ mixed methods to answer pertinent research questions. For instance, in *The New Black Politician* (Gillespie, forthcoming), my upcoming book on Black politics in Newark, I employ a number of varied tools (quantitative content analysis, descriptive and regression analysis of election returns, descriptive analysis of crime and unemployment data, in-depth interviews and ethnography) to answer questions about how young Black politicians challenge older Black politicians for power and what the consequences of those strategies are. Relying on only one type of data or one method of analysis would have been insufficient to fully answer the questions related to my chosen topic. Using a number of methods, though, helped to strengthen my argument.

I cannot stress enough the importance of respecting qualitative research methods. While I appreciate the generalizability of large-N, quantitative studies, there is something to be said for the depth of knowledge generated from a systematic and well-crafted qualitative study. Often, important details and insights can get lost in a sea of numbers. When done correctly, findings generated from qualitative methods such as interviews and ethnography should complement the results of large-N studies and help to generate better survey questions.

Why I Do It

I also value qualitative research for one important reason: it helps to keep me connected to real politics. Personally, I am appalled that some political scientists are so distracted by their research that they forget to engage real politics. Not only is it counterintuitive, but it also leads to shoddy scholarship. Disengaged scholarship is either externally invalid or underused. Either way, disconnection from real politics evinces a certain irrelevance that I am unwilling to accept in my own work.

Before taking my job at Emory, I spent a year working for a Democratic pollster in Washington. I would often have conversations with the managing partner of my firm in which we would talk about the differences between political scientists and political consultants. He would often warn me that the questions that I asked as a political scientist were interesting but not relevant to the needs of our clients, who included some of the biggest movers and shakers in Washington.

I have never forgotten those conversations. They spur me to remember that my research needs to have some type of real-world applicability. Thus, I view my role as a researcher as three-pronged. I have a responsibility to produce good scholarship and to advance academic debates. Related to that goal is my responsibility to teach students to think critically about race and politics in the hope that the knowledge I impart to them will have an impact on their behavior.

However, I also have a responsibility to politicians and the general public. As a scholar, I have the time to sit and think carefully and critically about campaign strategy and its policy implications. I have the time to examine issues systematically and synthesize findings in a coherent manner. Politicians should be able to turn to my research and gain insight about best practices or be challenged by the normative implications of my findings to alter their behavior. If these leaders find my work to be inaccessible or my questions irrelevant, then I have failed.

Similarly, my research findings should help illumine political matters for a general audience. We have the privilege of being able to explain government and politics to students and to a general audience. We should relish each and every opportunity to teach on a larger scale. Think about it. Who else can explain to voters how the median voter theorem affects candidate behavior in primaries and general elections? Where else are people going to learn about "rally around the flag" effects? It is our job to do this, and every time we cede this responsibility to the punditocracy, we make ourselves more and more irrelevant.

I think the concept of relevance is especially important for those of us who study race. We come from a community with serious entrenched problems that are getting worse on many dimensions. There is no time for abstract thought exercises. The entire Black community—elected officials and community members—needs the benefit of our study to help figure out what to do to reduce entrenched inequality.

Conclusion

Earlier this summer, I decided to adopt a new career mission statement: keeping the "politics" in "political science." This statement reminds me that I became a political scientist to answer important questions about politics, not arcane questions that appeal to only 10 people. Fulfilling this mission fits in nicely with the two W's and one H strategy outlined above. I generate research questions that are relevant to our understanding of Black politics; I let the question dictate the method and the data I use, and I always remember that my purpose in doing this research is to help my colleagues be better scholars; my students and the general public be better consumers of political information; and politicians be better campaigners and policy makers.

Note

*   Andra Gillespie is an Associate Professor, Emory University, Atlanta, GA.

References

Gillespie, Andra. ed. 2010. Whose Black Politics? Cases in Post-Racial Black Leadership. New York: Routledge.
———. Forthcoming. *The New Black Politician: Cory Booker, Newark and Post-Racial America.* New York. New York University Press.
King, Gary, Robert O. Keohane, and Sidney Verba. 1994. Designing Social Inquiry: Scientific Inference in Qualitative Research. Princeton, NJ: Princeton University Press.

Book Reviews

Examining the Context for the Obama Presidency: Book Reviews

The books reviewed in this issue of the *National Political Science Review* provide robust coverage of the *American Politics* subfield with special emphasis on gender politics, urban politics, minority politics, elections, public opinion, social and political movements, pedagogy and the political science curriculum, and the politics of higher education. Within the *Political Theory* subfield, the offerings raise critical questions about the coterminous origins of racism, imperialism, and gender constructs with liberalism, capitalism, the cultural logic of racial regimes for nation-building, and the epistemic role of African Gender Studies in African Studies. Finally, the reviews take up the question of what sense to make of the recent backlash against minority voting which has resulted in several states passing laws which prohibit free participation in the voting system in ways much too similar to the Post Reconstruction era after 1877. Within the *Comparative Politics* subfield, the reviews address racial politics in Brazil, education, the domain of knowledge with respect to race, gender, and class, in the context of colonial power relations in higher education, as well as the study of culture across the West African region and in South Africa.

The works chosen for review can be organized around four framing analytics. The first of these calls on readers to entertain the question of whether concepts such as incorporation and apathy are appropriate for explaining the way that minorities have entered the mainstream of American politics. Katherine Tate's *What's Going On? Political Incorporation and the Transformation of Black Public Opinion* (Georgetown University Press, Washington, DC, 2010), reviewed by D. Osei Robertson, and Jane Junn's and Kerry Haynie's *New Race Politics in America*: *Understanding Minority and Immigrant Politics* (Cambridge University Press, Cambridge, 2008), reviewed by Athena Mae King, provide clear-headed models of the framing analytic in these terms. Not only do they offer clues on how we might understand the range of civil rights, political mobilization, and social activism that created the foundation for Barack Obama's election, they also draw our attention to contemporary battlegrounds for Black Politics beyond Obama's election.

A second framing analytic turns our attention to the politics of knowledge and political theory. Thomas McCarthy's *Race, Empire, and the Idea of Human Development* (Cambridge University Press, New York, 2009), reviewed by Sherri Taylor, and Cedric Robinson's *Forgeries of Memory and Meaning: Blacks & the Regimes of Race in American Theater & Film before World War II* (University of North Carolina Press, Chapel Hill, NC, 2007), reviewed by Michael Tran, direct us toward longer historical trends that have produced hegemonic racial projects elaborated in the social sciences, social welfare professions, material and visual culture, and policy making. A striking example of what this analytic reveals is provided by Jason Brennan's *The Ethics of Voting* (Princeton University Press, Princeton, NJ, 2011), reviewed by Adam Harris. Brennan's principle interlocutor is what may be called, the *"racial logic of white vulnerability."* Never named explicitly as such, Brennan describes the legitimacy of White primaries, poll taxes, literacy tests—all the guarantees of White supremacist segregationist society, in a way that evokes questions about present-day efforts at minority voter suppression, and the stereotypical targeting of American Muslims and Americans with Spanish surnames as existing outside the legitimate boundaries of American citizenship. In this context knowing who now votes and their ethnic backgrounds are questions that have to be tied more openly to the many ideologies that emerge from White supremacy. Hence, this framing analytic highlights the manifestations of policy preferences, agendas, and political movements which emerged during the Obama Administration and whose assumptions must be constantly interrogated.

A third framing analytic directs us toward the groups that have embraced the Obama Presidency from the vantage point of being participants and heirs to the struggle for civil rights and racial justice. Tobin Miller Shearer's *Daily Demonstrations: The Civil Rights Movement in Mennonite Homes and Sanctuaries* (John Hopkins University Press, Baltimore, MD, 2010), reviewed by Charles Eagles, and Paula McClain's and Steven Tauber's *American Government in Black and White* (Paradigm, Boulder, CO, 2010), reviewed by Zahra Ahmed, encourage us to think about the claims being made by religious minorities and the youth of the twenty-first century on the history of the civil rights movement. In these works we are directed to the compelling evidence of Mennonite minister Vincent Harding's important work of leading the pro-civil rights defiance campaign within that religious community. Also we see contemporary youthful voters who identified with the Obama election campaign because of its capacity to talk about (without being only about) White supremacy and economic injustice. The forms which civic and community engagement take today are directly related to how we understand the political legacies of the 1960s' and 1970s' civil rights movements. Do we internalize renderings of that historical period as reductionist, non-oppositional, liberal, sanitizing, or blandly multiculturalist, or do we recognize the risks and dangers that ordinary people assumed for the sake of promoting change? The historical struggle for civil rights and racial justice is part of what is to be viewed as a potent resource for self-knowing in Rachelle Winkle-Wagner's *The Unchosen Me: Race, Gender, and Identity Among Black Women in College* (Johns Hopkins University Press, Baltimore, MD, 2009), reviewed by Taisha Caldwell. Winkle-Wagner raises nettlesome questions about the persistent political ramifications of demonizing Black female excellence and leadership in higher education during the Obama Presidency era.

A fourth and final framing analytic concerns the intersection of place and identity in the formation of distinctly political identities. Place and identity intersect in cities, regions, and nation-states are captured in two edited collections under review. Darnell Hunt and Ana-Christina Ramon, editors of *Black Los Angeles: American Dreams and Racial Realities* (New York University Press, New York 2010), reviewed by Rick Moss, Director and Curator of the African American Museum and Library at Oakland, provide a vivid picture of the importance of the study of Black Politics in terms of community or ethos. This framing analytic is echoed in Bernd Reiter and Gladys L. Mitchell's *Brazil's New Racial Politics* (Lynne Reinner, Boulder, CO, 2009) reviewed by Kia Lilly-Caldwell. Paying special attention to political movements, electoral campaigns, the development of Black voting blocks, and Black women as shapers of urban policy, the contributors to this volume point to the widest possible range of Black consciousness to be found across institutionalized and informal politics. Scholars of gender politics, comparative politics, and the African Diaspora politics will find the collections reviewed by Audrey Kim of particular interest. Reitumetse Mabokela and Zine Magubane have edited *Hear Our Voices: Race, Gender, and the Status of Black South African Women in the Academy* (University of South Africa Press/Koninklijke Brill, Pretoria/Leiden, 2004), which is considered a major contribution to Black women's studies in South Africa. It examines the institutional legacies of racial segregation in higher education and finds that overall compliance with new affirmative action policies has faced a severe backlash. The editors provide a compelling history of the construction of racial regimes in which post-apartheid politics in South Africa is being played out. Similarly, but with a far wider scope, Oyèrónké Oyĕwùmí', editor of *African Gender Studies: A Reader* (Palgrave Macmillan, New York, 2005), places a range of research within the context of the strains that the Eurocentric politics of knowledge places on traditional West African family structures. Works such as this one remind us that much of the work in the study of Black Politics starts from the premise that common international links join Black people whose communities were forged through their resistance to White supremacy emanating from the projection and maintenance of an American empire.

One final word about the NPSR Book Review section. By design, the Book Review section is intended to reach out to the widest possible readership of those concerned with the growth and sustainability of the life of Black politics. These include academics (and naturally the members of the National Conference of Black Political Scientists), community activists and the clergy, political practitioners, campaign consultants, independent scholars, elected officials, and educators. The Book Review section makes an effort to enlarge this readership space by reviewing books which cut across disciplines and fields of political science. And, since our main focus is on Black political life in all of its dimensions, we invite reviews and reviewers who come from different locations in the conduct and analysis of the Black political experience. We hope that our readers find merit in our expansive view of the Black political experience.

Tiffany Willoughby-Herard
University of California, Irvine

Brennan, Jason. *The Ethics of Voting* (Princeton, NJ: Princeton University Press, 2011), $29.95, 222 pp. ISBN: 978-0-691-14481-8 (cloth).

With the 2012 U.S. Presidential election imminent and political posturing at its peak, Jason Brennan's *The Ethics of Voting* is a timely assessment in voting theory. At base, the work aims to answer the major questions of voting theory and, ultimately, answer the question of how citizens should operate in voting. Brennan offers the provocative suggestion that citizens ought not vote when they are not "good" at voting and even in the event that one does cast a good vote, if there is no sufficient justification for that vote, the citizen should have abstained from voting.

Essentially, what Brennan aims to do is formulate a Universalist position that is applicable to all those operating in the democratic system of voting. His position further suggests that citizens should not vote when they are voting from (1) immoral beliefs, (2) epistemic irrationality, and (3) ignorance. Before engaging these suggestions, however, it is necessary to consider democracy as it stands in order to adequately assess how voting ought to be practiced properly in the United States and other democratic nations.

Indeed, voting in the United States has a history of disproportionate disenfranchisement. Blacks have been consistently subject to policies that bar them from voting and violent attacks if they actually voted. The history of suppression of the Black voter teaches us important things about the nature and uniqueness of voting to democracy. The publishing of Brennan's work is situated in a place in history where the institution of voting is again coming under attack with several policies that negatively affect Blacks and others operating in the system. Though voter ID laws are being presented in most of the fifty states under the guise of preventing voter fraud, they are being fought. The NAACP is standing alongside Fayette County, Georgia voters in their federal lawsuit claiming disenfranchisement in at-large elections, and challenging widespread characterizations of the civil rights movement as more peaceful than it was. In this context, is Brennan's suggestion that people should not vote, serving a purpose beyond positing that people should not vote badly?

This question is answered by the book's subtle suggestions, such as that there are moral standards in voting. While this seems to be a just suggestion by ethical standards, that most people would agree with, Brennan further poses the questions: "Why not have a poll exam—a test of competence that determines whether a citizen may vote? Or why not give extra votes to educated people, as Britain did until 1949?" (7). Questions such as these violate the deep history of Black voting in American Democracy.

Former Republican Congressman Tom Tancredo, in February 2010 at a Tea Party rally, suggested that citizens should be subject to "civics-literacy" tests before they should be able to vote. Tancredo came under fire because of the history of disenfranchisement by means of literacy tests that Blacks suffered through until the passing of the Voting Rights Act of 1965. These tests were implemented by White supremacists in order to keep Blacks from participating in elections. Furthermore, Brennan's suggestion that educated people should have more votes veers far too closely to disenfranchising practices.

Brennan does not "regard it as self-evident that we have a natural right to political equality" (6). However, the implicit suggestion in Brennan's work is that everyone operating in American Democracy is placed on an even plateau and thus should operate the same way. When viewed in proper historical context, it is evident that citizens of the United States are not beginning at the same place, as far as historical enfranchisement and the Black response to disenfranchisement is concerned.[1] This neglect of history places Brennan's book in a position that is not able to adequately assess the situation of Blacks in the United States and thus not able to make assertions about the ethical features of Blacks voting. Indeed, this is a work in political philosophy that aims to paint the world as it ought to be; however, Brennan has produced a work that is not practically applicable—it cannot that is to say, it cannot serve a practical function in common democracy because of its neglect of history.

The Ethics of Voting is hailed as a progressive work in democratic thought; however, given the vitality of voting to Democracy, and how each vote shapes democracy, this work can be viewed as explicitly anti-democratic. One of its central implications is that uninformed voters somehow deform democratic structures and lead to unjust policies. By taking a look at the educational system, and "orthodox" forms of civics-literacy socialization, it is evident that Blacks and other minority groups are not typically afforded a civics education which socializes them into meaningful political action. However, recent literature on contemporary Black youth political involvement, such as Andreana Clay's *The Hip-Hop Generation Fights Back: Youth, Activism, and Post-Civil Rights Politics* (New York University Press, New York, 2012), Cathy Cohen's *Democracy Remixed: Black Youth and the Future of American Politics* (Oxford University Press, Oxford, 2010), and Kimala Price's essay "Hip-Hop Feminism at the Political Crossroads: Organizing for Reproductive Justice and Beyond" in *Home Girls Make Some Noise!* (Parker, Mira Loma, CA, 2007) demonstrate that young Black voters gain their political education via other means. In this regard, the idea of an "informed" voter assumes a new definition that is not touched on by Brennan. With this in mind, can there ever be an assumption that one is not informed enough to vote? What constitutes proper information toward casting a *good* vote?

Brennan assumes that all citizens who cast ballots should vote for the benefit of the common good, stating, "Voters should justifiedly believe that the policies or candidates they support would promote the common good. Otherwise, they should abstain from voting" (91). This assumption slips into a mold that suggests there is a *best* policy for all; however, there is not necessarily a policy that is beneficial for all; therefore, the suggestion must be viewed as utilitarian. In the utilitarian view, the search is for a policy that provides the greatest benefit for the majority and risks degenerating into a tyranny of the majority. Blacks in the United States have suffered through policies which do great benefits for a White majority, but systematically disenfranchise Black people. In voting, one such example is all-White Democratic primary elections which were reinforced by state law until several legal cases, such as *Nixon v. Herndon (1927),* set precedent, stating that such primary elections violated the Fourteenth Amendment. These policies were harmful to Blacks yet they served an advantageous purpose for Whites. Brennan's work is not in a proper position to assess how Blacks should vote because the "common good" for minority populations may not be the same as it is for Whites operating in American Democracy.

This book succeeds in creating an arena to look at voting ethically and poses several questions which could be useful in ultimately formulating a code of ethics for voters. However, the the conclusions drawn in *The Ethics of Voting* fail with regard to several minority groups, especially Blacks, based on historical disenfranchisement. In this respect, it leaves much to be desired.

Note

1. For an account of Black responses to systemic barriers specific to voting and party politics, see Gurin, Patricia, Shirley Hatchett, and James S. Jackson. *Hope and independence: Blacks' Response to Electoral and Party Politics*. New York: R. Sage Foundation, 1989.

Adam M. Harris
Alabama A&M University

Junn, Jane and Kerry L. Haynie, eds. *New Race Politics in America: Understanding Minority and Immigrant Politics* (New York: Cambridge University Press, 2008), $26.99, 208 pp. ISBN: 978-0-52185-427-6 (paper).

The results of the 2010 U.S. Census reflect substantial growth in the minority and immigrant population over the past decade. According to the census, individuals of Latino descent represented the largest increase in the U.S. population, growing approximately 43 percent in the decade. (By comparison, the nation's overall population increased by 9.7 percent in the same time frame.) Other minority groups also experienced considerable growth during this period: African American numbers increased from 12.32 percent to 12.6 percent and the Asian population increased from 4 percent to 4.8 percent. This increase in minority group numbers, arising primarily from immigration, has changed the landscape of many states in terms of racial and ethnic makeup; invariably, this shift in demographic complexion will be accompanied by changes in the electorate. The significance of this shift has come to the attention of the country as a whole; to date, several states, led by Arizona, have promulgated legislation designed to curtail immigration (particularly from neighboring Mexico), and population projections show that native-born Whites will lose their majority status in less than forty years. Though scholars have addressed changes in the racial dynamic and moved the conversation from "black and white" to multiracial and multicultural in the past decade or so, issues of race and ethnicity in the political realm foretell new implications for policy preferences, policy actors, and political institutions.

Confronting the changes in the electorate is the central tenet in *New Race Politics in America*. This book is a compilation of research by political science scholars (edited by Jane Junn and Kerry Haynie) which collectively addresses the notion that the political landscape is being reshaped by the rising tide of immigration and the increase in the overall minority population. Collectively, the research covers three themes: (1) strategies to mobilize citizens into politics vis-à-vis political parties, political elites, candidate advertisements, and co-ethnic outreach efforts; (2) the degree of racial consciousness and sense of "linked fate" among members of racial and ethnic groups; and (3) the degree to which conventional models of political behavior are applicable to U.S. minority populations. To date, definitive answers as to how this change will affect the political process, the existing major parties, and policy preferences of the electorate are unanswered. However, the authors are successful in bringing to the fore the fact that these questions will have to be addressed—and answers provided—in the near future.

Kristi Andersen analyzes the degree to which political parties will seek to incorporate immigrants into American democracy. Historically, political parties have sought to weave immigrants into the fabric of the party (via the "party machines" of the Democrats) or used nativist sentiments to prevent their inclusion (e.g., the "Know Nothings"). Andersen argues political institutions will seek immigrant incorporation if it is in their best strategic interests to do; if so, several contextual factors must be considered, including state of residence, rates of citizenship, and the presence of civic and social organizations. She finds that on the whole, both of the major parties (on the national level) lack the incentive to engage in large-scale incorporation of immigrant groups, particularly in non-competitive states; however, both parties show occasional deference to immigrant groups by utilizing (mostly symbolic and occasionally material) outreach efforts. It will be beneficial for future research to revisit these issues in the context of 2012 redistricting and state action regarding immigration (e.g., Arizona, South Carolina, and other states that have since promulgated rather stringent immigration reform measures); as such, immigrant mobilization may increase across the board in response to proposed immigration reforms and new policies put into place by these and other states. (Also, given the increasing political polarization of the past decade, one would surmise that parties will pursue or reject increased numbers from minority/immigrant groups based on the issue at hand—for example, Republicans will be loath to pursue the Mexican American vote in states passing and enforcing stricter immigration laws and E-verify for employment and refer to any immigration programs besides their own as "amnesty.")

Dennis Chong and Dukhong Kim examine whether the concept of "linked fate" (belief that one's success or failure is tied to one's racial group as a whole) is as important for Latinos and Asian Americans as it is for African Americans. They find that unlike African Americans, Latinos and Asian Americans' views regarding economic status and discrimination are more likely to be based on personal experiences than with the racial/ethnic group as a whole. This finding is justifiable considering that the authors highlight a major weakness in their conclusion, namely, the grouping of all Latinos together, though they are an ethnic group and can be of any race. As such, Latino perceptions may be colored to an extent by their White/non-White status (which also, to an extent shapes their political leanings. For instance, Latinos who identify racially as "white" may be more conservative than those who are "nonwhite." This has been shown in states such as Florida, which has a large Cuban population which consistently votes conservative/Republican in large numbers). Similar issues arise in studies which group Asian Americans together without much consideration to the ethnic and or racial differences.

Janelle Wong, Pei-Te Lien, and M. Margaret Conway address this notion of Asian ethnic differences in their study and argue Asian Americans will vary in terms of political participation partly as a consequence of their ethnicities. Using both traditional factors (socioeconomic status, psychological engagement, and institutional connections) and nontraditional, Asian American-specific factors relating to "linked fate" (e.g., personal discrimination, participation in and advocacy of Asian American causes, and ethnic origin), the authors find that while traditional factors may explain Asian American participation, other factors have varying degrees of influence on political participation outside of voting, namely, that South Asian Americans and Vietnamese Americans (when compared to Chinese Americans) are more likely to engage in political participation beyond voting; however, individuals who are foreign-born or educated outside of the United States are less likely to engage in similar activities. As such, targeting the Asian American community for mobilization purposes will be difficult, given its ethnic diversity.

Rodolfo O. De La Garza, Marisa A. Abrajano, and Jeronimo Cortina's analysis of co-ethnic mobilization and Latino turnout suggests direct contact with the Latino community by both Latino and non-Latino activists resulted in Latino mobilization and turnout for the 2000 Presidential election on a national scale. The authors also find that in states with the highest Latino populations (California, Florida, Illinois, New York, and Texas), each state had a different concentration of a particular Latino ethnic group and these groups were mobilized (internally or externally) based on the state's degree of competitiveness in the upcoming election along with political incidences which directly affected the Latino community (i.e., actions taken by the Clinton Administration regarding the Elian Gonzalez case in Florida and Navy bombing exercises on the island of Vieques, issues which affected the Cuban and Puerto Rican populations, respectively). However, the authors were unsure as to why there is a mixed effect of ethnicity and being contacted by both Latinos and non-Latinos to vote in different states; one could speculate that the factors which address participation among Asian Americans in Wong et al.'s research are applicable in this piece as well.

Victoria M. DeFrancesco Soto and Jennifer L. Merolla's contribution finds that Latino voting behavior is directly influenced by mass media communication (e.g., television ads) geared specifically toward Latinos; interestingly, political commercials carried out in English and specifically targeting Latinos increase the probability of voting for Latinos who primarily speak Spanish than general advertisements. At the same time, however, the advertisements had no significant effect on Latinos whose primary language was English. Like De La Garza et al., the authors used data which disaggregated Latinos into particular ethnic groups and emphasized media markets with signficant Latino populations. The findings suggest that, like Asian Americans, a "one size fits all" strategy for mobilizing Latino voters in future mobilization efforts will be insufficient, as varying degrees of acculturation are correlated with Latino mobilization. So far, a phenomenon no scholar has addressed to this point (but will be interesting to see nonetheless) is the utilization of (or potential challenges to using) the Voting Rights Act for mobilization purposes, in particular, emphasizing section 203 which provides registration and voting information in the native language of minority groups covered under it (including Spanish-speaking Latinos).

Frederick Harris, Brian D. McKenzie, and Valeria Sinclair-Chapman address Black political participation in the post-Civil Rights Era using a macro model (which examines participation as a group phenomenon). The authors determine that using individual-level data to explain Black political participation is insufficient, as it assumes data collected from a few subjects (taken in isolation and at different points in time) is reflective of the political behavior for the entire Black population (which, contrary to popular belief, is not monolithic). Using the Roper Social and Political Trends data set and Composite Participation, Political Work and Organizational Work Participation Indices from 1973–1993 and examining variables related to civic participation beyond voting, the authors found considerable volatility in collective Black activism and participation over this period, with the greatest rates of participation in 1976, 1984–1985, the lowest rates in 1980 and 1990, and variances between the extremes in all other years. The authors argue that gains and losses in Black empowerment may be influenced by exogenous social and economic factors which alternately empower and hamper Black communities; however, the authors go into very little detail as to why certain years are significant for strong or weak participation. (For example: Black voters were, ostensibly, motivated to participate more in 1976 due to the presidential candidacy of Jimmy Carter and in 1984 because of Jesse Jackson; less participation occurred in the late 1980s and 1990s because of the strong candidacies of Ronald Reagan, George Bush, the growing number of Republican candidates for office at the national, state, and local levels during this period, and the effects of economic downturns on African Americans during this period.) The authors reference social interaction and Black "political entrepreneurs" as key factors in stimulating Black activism at the aggregate level. However, a discussion of these factors in connection with the data findings is lacking; perhaps its inclusion would provide greater explanation for the dynamic changes in Black participation during this twenty-year period.

Paula D. McClain, Victoria M. De Francesco Soto et al. investigate the influence of Black political "elites" on prospective Latino voters in Durham, North Carolina (one of the fastest-growing areas of the country, particularly for Latinos). The authors contend that the Black–White paradigm which is *de rigueur* in Southern states will invariably change due to the influx of Latino immigrants; therefore, the degree to which Black Southerners will be affected by this demographic change, Black attitudes toward Latinos (in terms of economics and policy preferences), and whether the "Black elite" will intervene on behalf of and advocate for the policy preferences of the Latino community are issues of concern. Using a telephone survey (for the masses) and face-to-face interviews (for the elites), the authors found that elites who interacted primarily with other elites did not perceive any tensions between Blacks and Latinos; however, elites who interacted primarily with the masses were aware of tensions between the two groups. The authors also found that Blacks who hold jobs—but at lower salaries—were less likely to feel positive about Black/Latino relations, whereas unemployed Blacks or Blacks with higher incomes were more likely to feel positive about said relations. These findings suggest that Black/Latino relations in Durham are tentative, but somewhat favorable. The arrival of Latinos to the South in large numbers is a relatively new phenomenon; therefore, this study represents a good starting point for examining the future impact of Latino presence on race/ethnic relations in this region.

This collection of articles regarding minority and immigrant politics is an important first step to understanding the changing dynamics of the country's demographic makeup and the implications it will have on the political system. The authors are successful in moving the political conversation beyond Black and White while addressing potential difficulties that may be encountered by political institutions in mobilizing—or failing to recognize and mobilize—potential new voters. Given the latest Census figures and current redistricting efforts in state legislatures, one would surmise that racial/ethnic/minority interests and policy preferences will come to the fore, particularly in states which saw strong increases in immigration over the past decade. Finally, the articles raise as many questions as they seek to answer; however, one overarching question remains: Is it incumbent upon existing players and institutions in the political realm to expand the role of identity politics in future elections, or does the onus of participation sit squarely on the shoulders of racial/minority/immigrant groups?

Athena M. King
University of South Carolina

Mabokela, Reitumetse and Zine Magubane, eds. *Hear Our Voices: Race, Gender, and the Status of Black South African Women in the Academy* (Pretoria/Leiden: University of South Africa Press/Koninklijke Brill, 2004), $30.00, 120 pp. ISBN: 1-8688-294-2 (paper).

Oyĕwùmí', Oyèrónké, ed. *African Gender Studies: A Reader* (New York: Palgrave Macmillan, 2005), $34.00, 448 pp. ISBN: 1-4039-6283-9 (paper).

In the anthologies *Hear Our Voices* and *African Gender Studies: A Reader*, the authors address the epistemological and pedagogical impediments blighting scholarship about the African continent and creating institutional friction for African female academics. A key frame for thinking about the politics of knowledge and gender studies in Africa is what I have come to call "theory as inseminated reality" which figures African female scholars in a dangerous nexus of Eurocentric academic filiation. While the *African Gender Studies* authors specifically deconstruct the Eurocentric hegemony within theories of race, culture, gender, and identity, the authors in *Hear Our Voices* reveal how those theories are institutionalized as dominant ideologies discursively affecting female scholars at South African universities. Taken together, this powerful dynamic of theory in practice reinforces the authors' charge to critically and historically contextualize phenomena occurring at instrumental moments of change. The potency of apartheid's half-life in "liberal" universities is compounded by sexist notions of academic integrity that in turn stunt the vigor of African female scholars. Consequently, the disregard and exclusion of Black women in academia as actors and subjects has continued the hidden curriculum of higher education which remains nestled in the co-optive thrust of nineteenth-century Eurocentrism and patriarchy. The resulting cultural imperialism in higher education has thus undermined the post-apartheid laws to change the academy and engendered hostility for African feminist scholarship challenging Western assumptions of Africa's societal realities.

In her analysis of how the Eurocentric gaze, sometimes described in postmodern psychoanalytic texts as "scopophilia," produces misinterpretations and mischaracterizations of societal problems, Oyèrónké Oyĕwùmí's chapter in *African Gender Studies*, "Visualizing the Body: Western Theories and African Subjects," complements Zine Magubane's critique of universities' institutional culture in "A Pigment of the Imagination? Race, Subjectivity, Knowledge and the Image of the Black Intellectual" in *Hear Our Voices*. Oyĕwùmí argues that since Western thought is fundamentally grounded in the visual sense, the biological differences in bodies are understood as hierarchical markers of civility and progress. This cultural logic of sight, therefore, provokes a reality that accepts race as its central organizing principle of society, and gender as its defining ontological mechanism for social roles. She critiques this Western cultural logic as bio-logic in terms of its imposition on non-Western models of society, specifically how the gender framework was deployed in studies of Yorùbá culture as a means to make sense of their sophisticated non-gendered kinship structures. Magubane's criticism of the problematic of visual sense bio-logic confronts how "the 'alienating culture' of the contemporary South African university can be comprehended as a direct consequence of the social forces that shaped it historically. African academics continue to be stereotyped and represented in ways that implicitly recall the 'School Kaffir' image—[that Africans will assert competence when they have none]—promulgated at the turn of the century" (Magubane 51). Such classic stereotypes and tropes about Black scholars operate at the visual level to fragment and destroy the groundings and insights which Black female scholars are calling upon when designing and conducting research. Oyěwùmí points to the ways that "academics have become one of the most effective international hegemonizing forces, producing not homogenous social experiences but a homogeny of hegemonic forces" (Oyěwùmí 12) thus re-entrenching colonial discourse within universities. Not only do these scholars attend to the imposition of Western theories but they examine the context in which liberal policies of diversity have come to be convenient corporate stand-ins for human freedom and thus create a toxic environment for female African scholars who must confront epistemological and pedagogical patriarchy and racism in pursuing their research and establishing their professional worth. These contradictions and frictions embody the very battlefield of Western intellectual insemination and post-colonial realities keeping universities from a meaningful transformation, as well as being meaningful vehicles for social change.

Ifi Amadiume's chapter, "Theorizing Matriarchy in Africa: Kinship Ideologies and Systems in Africa and Europe" in *African Gender Studies* further underscores the paradoxes and contradictions inherent in Cheryl-Ann Potgieter and Anne-Gloria Senkgane Moleko's chapter in *Hear Our Voices*, "Stand Out, Stand Up, Move Out: Experiences of Black South African Women at Historically White Universities." Potgieter and Senkgane Moleko document the experiences of Black female scholars having to take on the maternal role at universities—among students and colleagues; while being denied the leadership and decision-making authority of matrifocality, a significant and foundational social formation in African communities. Amadiume argues that gendered Eurocentric ideologies about the politics of knowledge and how one conducts research manifest as norms which disavow the importance of womb symbolism and matriarchy in African cultural and social constructions; and in turn leads her to question dominant representations of historical events by considering which histories should in fact contextualize these events. Furthermore, the post-apartheid South African universities' knowledge production, development, and dissemination echo these same epistemological and pedagogical norms by expecting Black academics "to adopt the 'ways of doing' and 'knowing' of their white institutions, with little reciprocal change on the part of the institution" (Amadiume 96; Potgieter, Senkgane Moleko 85).

The chapter by Obioma Nnaemeka in *African Gender Studies*, "Bringing African Women into the Classroom: Rethinking Pedagogy and Epistemology" develops the idea of transforming the academy in Pumla Gqola's chapter on "Language and Power, Languages of Power: A Black Woman's Journey through Three South African Universities" in *Hear Our Voices*. In her study of cross-cultural pedagogy, Nnaemkea emphasizes humility, attention to intentionality, perspective, and positionality for outsiders and global feminist solidarity through transgression rather than a crossover so as to avoid personal cultural bias. She calls for a global feminist solidarity that is mutually liberating through a re-examination of the construction of knowledge and qualifications for binding sisterhood. Nnaemkea addresses this as an opportunity for women's self-knowledge in raising consciousness of our own oppression as means for wider identification and collaboration against Eurocentric structures of patriarchy. Gqola, on the other hand, more critically focuses on how, within an illusory myth of the rainbow society, the universities "are not the cerebral uncontaminated spaces they are believed to be;" and how their "hidden curriculum serves to undermine the reconceptualization of the systems of knowledge production, as well as a meaningful engagement with the discourses of Africa and participation in the formulation of how Africa registers in the world" (Gqola 27, 34). Gqola's teaching model is "one which works to 'argue that being implicated in the relations of power does not preclude subversion or engaging in acts that push beyond a given order of things'" (Gqola 37). This marginal position is where she seeks to build global feminist solidarity and yet cautions against the power of Eurocentric academic discourse because "even if we recognize that margins offer dynamic activism at times, we must be wary of occupying margins in a manner that ghettoizes our voices in ways which are anything but subversive" (Gqola 38). These two authors are concerned with how knowledge production and dissemination affect the solidarity of women. They interrogate the negative space that women scholars occupy at the university as teachers and researchers while offering different teaching styles for promoting solidarity. Nnaemkea suggests a methodological approach of teaching connections and "thereby reducing the distance between the student and the foreign culture and increasing points of interaction and identification" and "requires that we grasp and teach sameness and difference simultaneously" (Nnaemkea 60, 64).

Hear Our Voices and *African Gender Studies* dynamically reveal how African female scholars' work and communities are compromised in the universities' policies and patriarchal cultures, which, ultimately threaten post-apartheid laws. These anthologies thus demonstrate not only the potency of colonial hegemony in African universities, but also how the African female scholarship can offer a specific and substantive critique of the political and academic efficacy of post-racial intentions and knowledge projects in the university.

Audrey Kim
University of California, Irvine

Shearer, Tobin Miller. *Daily Demonstrations: The Civil Rights Movement in Mennonite Homes and Sanctuaries* (Baltimore, MD: Johns Hopkins University Press, 2010), $65.00, 392 pp. ISBN: 978-0-80189-700-9 (cloth).

Religion's importance to the African American freedom struggle has never been doubted; many scholars have viewed it as essentially a religious movement. The vast literature on the civil rights movement includes many studies of churches, religion, and individuals. In addition to innumerable books on the religious ideas, rhetoric and preaching style, and faith of Martin Luther King, Jr., the scholarship has examined the roles of other religious figures such as the Reverend Fred Shuttlesworth and southern rabbis; specific denominations including Baptists, Methodists, Presbyterians, and Episcopalians; and various religious organizations ranging from the National Council of Churches to the Southern Christian Leadership Conference. Important group studies have also examined the southern White clergy's relationship to the movement and religion's impact on activists in Mississippi. Historians have even debated the importance of religion in segregationist arguments against the civil rights movement.

To this growing scholarship Tobin Miller Shearer adds a careful, compassionate, but critical study of the Mennonites and the civil rights movement from 1918 to 1971. It appears as a volume in the Young Center Books in Anabaptist and Pietist Studies. At the outset, Shearer, himself a Mennonite and social activist, provides the uninformed with important background information on the Mennonites. According to Shearer, "these Anabaptist heirs of the sixteenth-century Radical Reformation" came to America in the late seventeenth century (xiv). After declaring that he chose two Mennonite denominations for his study, Shearer explains the significant differences between the (Old) Mennonite Church and the General Conference Mennonite Church. The former had a more hierarchical organization with stronger bishops and adhered more strictly to church doctrines. It was strongest on the East coast, particularly in Pennsylvania and Virginia, and its members encountered Blacks in cities and in the South. The (Old) Mennonite Church's nearly 90,000 members by 1970, came mainly from a Germanic-Swiss background. On the other hand, the fewer than 40,000 members of the General Conference Mennonite Church had Prussian and southern Russian roots and were centered in rural communities of the Midwest, especially in Nebraska and Kansas, where they had little contact with African Americans. Less highly structured, the General Conference Mennonite Churches contained a wider variety of theological perspectives.

In their relationship with the civil rights movement, Shearer identifies three tensions among the Mennonites. First, though committed to nonresistance, they had to oppose the movement's nonviolent demonstrations. Second, Mennonites had opposed slavery and endorsed racial equality, but they had little contact with Blacks. Third, as nonconformists, they separated themselves from the larger contaminated society, yet they wanted to assist African Americans. The tensions caused Mennonites to debate how they could maintain their religious views and support the civil rights movement. In every case, they struggled to protect their "reputations as racial egalitarians while promoting nonresistance and nonconformity" (xvi).

The opening survey chapter divides the Mennonites' historical relationship with race into six stages. After supporting the segregationist status quo, in 1945 Mennonites gained their first ordained Black minister and in the late forties began to evangelize Blacks. In the early 1950s Mennonites intervened more directly for racial equality while also trying to maintain their cultural separatism. From 1956 to 1962, Shearer contends, the Mennonites experienced their greatest "promise for the hope of racial integration and the possibility of fresh engagement with racial justice" (17). In the mid-1960s, some Mennonites participated in political activism, but intense internal debates over the church and civil rights persisted. Black Power produced "a sense of dislocation and, at times, betrayal" among Mennonites (25). According to Shearer, a majority of Mennonites may not yet have supported integration. Throughout the changes in the twentieth century, the Mennonites' racial values closely resembled those of the larger culture.

Six rich and detailed chapters present case studies of a variety of specific incidents, individuals, and activities involving the Mennonites and civil rights. According to Shearer, through an interracial friendship beginning in the 1930s, Rowena Lark and Fannie Swartzenruber opposed segregation in the church; as "culturally creative resisters," they used "common religious resources like clothing and ritual to protest racial exclusion"(59, 31). The book's longest chapter explores four stories from 1950 to 1971 involving both the (Old) Mennonite Church's Fresh Air program, that brought urban Black children for short visits with rural White Mennonite families, and the General Conference's work at Camp Landon in Mississippi to take Blacks to similar homes in the Midwest. As "intimate disruptions" of ordinary lives, the "often racially naive" Fresh Air programs sought to undermine racial segregation by exposing prejudice and by creating relationship among children (63, 65). An important chapter examines the well-known minister, activist, and scholar, Vincent Harding. His attempts to "straddle the border between traditional Mennonite quietism and civil rights activism" exerted a "unique influence" on the church on racial issues from 1958 to 1966 (99). According to Shearer, the Black Mennonite minister "shaped the Mennonite church's response to the Second Reconstruction" more than any other individual (99). After pushing his church toward activism, a frustrated Harding left the Mennonites in the late 1960s. Shearer examines the marriage of Annabelle Conrad and Gerald Hughes to reveal how Mennonite attitudes toward interracial unions changed from 1930 to 1971. Though "the topic of interracial marriage troubled White Mennonites for a longer period, it proved more difficult to discuss, and involved fewer appeals to scripture," the author contends, "Mennonite leaders came to support interracial marriage by the end of the 1960s" (133). Shearer explores the integration of local congregations through the different experiences of two Chicago churches; Woodlawn stressed civil rights and by 1971 had closed, while Community stressed community service and succeeded. In the last substantive chapter, Shearer describes how Mennonites responded to Black Power and demands for reparations.

In Shearer's view the Mennonites' history of activism reveals a civil rights story significantly different from the conventional account. Even in his focus on the church, Shearer declares, "The church was not just a staging ground for civil rights activity; it was also a site of civil rights activity" (226). With their contributions occurring away from publicity in their private homes and church sanctuaries, Shearer argues for a wider conception of civil rights protest that includes "congregational walkouts, integration visitations, distinctive attire, and structured seminars within religious groups" (232). In addition, Mennonite resistance did not depend on charismatic men because women and children played key roles. The Mennonite story "also challenges the primacy of legislative strategies" for change (226). Though individual Mennonites did lobby for passage of the Civil Rights Act of 1964 and the Voting Rights Act of 1965, Shearer shows how Mennonites stressed personal relationships and "fostered intimate contact across racial lines" ahead of the courts and congress (226). At the same time, he recognizes religion's powerful influence both in support of the movement and in opposition to it. Finally, the Mennonites' emphasis on ordinary events "flattens out the civil rights timeline" because the story of their "daily demonstrations" deemphasizes the traditional heroic Montgomery-to-Memphis narrative (233).

Though Shearer successfully rescues the Mennonite civil rights story, he may overstate his case for the importance of their "daily demonstrations." Not only does he argue that Mennonites proved disproportionately influential across the nation," but he compares the Mennonite demonstrators with the more conventional civil rights protestors (xvii). The Mennonites "displayed courage equal to that of demonstrators who faced fire hoses and police dogs" (ix) Their "internal acts [in homes and sanctuaries] required the same kind of long-term commitment, relational depth, and strategic creativity displayed in the most successful public campaigns of the civil rights movement" (233). Similarly, in the interpretive struggle between the national and local movements, between top-down and bottom-up social change, Shearer exaggerates the importance of the Mennonite experience. Despite his claims, his narrative, like their activism, lacks drama. Though laudable, their modest daily protests struggle to sustain the story for 250 often repetitious pages.

Based on the Mennonites' civil rights history, Shearer does sensibly suggest additional subjects for study. He notes, for example, that scholars need to pursue the differences and influences between city and country. The relationship between the state and the church also warrants more careful analysis, as does the division between the sacred and the secular. Not only should students of the movement appreciate Shearer's study of the Mennonites and want to pay attention to his claims for a new civil rights history, they also should consider his proposals for further research.

Charles W. Eagles
University of Mississippi

Tate, Katherine. *What's Going On? Political Incorporation and the Transformation of Black Public Opinion* (Washington, DC: Georgetown University Press, 2010), $29.95, 208 pp. ISBN: 978-1-58901-702-3 (paper).

What's Going On? Political Incorporation and the Transformation of Black Public Opinion by Katherine Tate is an intriguing work drawing together more than thirty years of public opinion data from a variety of sources. She posits that over this period public opinion among Blacks has become more moderate on a number of political issues, which Tate primarily attributes to changes in Black leadership. "This Black opinion shift," Tate contends, "is based on the transformation of African American politics, away from radical challenges to the political status quo toward inclusive, bipartisan electoral politics" (2). She notes that the post Civil Rights/Black Power leadership cadre is an incorporated class (particularly in the Democratic Party) and their systemic inclusion is "a key explanatory factor in the moderation of Black public opinion" (9). Tate contends that as the Democratic Party has become more centrist in its orientation, Blacks have followed this same trajectory. Moreover, she espouses that this shift is "more enduring than temporary" (4). Tate examines Black public opinion on a number of issues that have defined the political landscape for decades, including: welfare reform, crime, government support for Blacks and minorities, education policies, immigration, and U.S. foreign policy. To validate her argument, the author examines various academic and media surveys to demonstrate the temporal moderation of Black public opinion on several key issues. She then links this shift to political elites through numerous regression analyses.

One of the first issues that Tate explores is African American support for welfare reform and government assistance. Using the 1996 NBES (National Black Election Study), she found that a majority of Blacks favored welfare reform and employing mean scores from the ANES (American National Election Study) cumulative file she illustrates how support for food stamps and welfare decreased among Blacks from 1984 to 2004 (18, 30). To understand this decline in support for government aid, the author conducts a regression analysis of support for Clinton's welfare reform proposal. In line with her central thesis that Black leadership influences public opinion, the author includes the independent variables (all thermometers) Jesse Jackson, CBC, and Bill Clinton in her model (21–23). The strongest predictor in her model was the "common fate" variable which had a negative effect on support for welfare reform, while the "black women common fate" variable predicted the most significant effect. In this model, there is only nominal support of the author's central thesis.

Expanding on this issue of government assistance to Blacks, Tate also explores how African American views on affirmative action have shifted over time using Time/CNN (1991) and NBES (1984–1988, 1996) data sets. Her regression models revealed "that the primary variables significantly related to Black support for affirmative action pertain to their perceptions of the degree to which Blacks remain victimized by racial stereotypes and discrimination" (52). The leadership variables (Bill Clinton and NAACP thermometers) were statistically significant, but were far less robust than the racial stereotypes or discrimination variable. Another area the author explores is African American views on immigration. She posits that "Black opinion on immigration flows is relatively stable, with a majority to a plurality endorsing the position that immigration numbers should be reduced" (117). In general, Tate found that African American opinion on immigration mirrored the views of Whites, with Blacks being slightly more liberal in many instances. To gauge this support the author conducted a regression analysis finding that the only significant variable was "homeownership" (Black homeowners supported immigration less), and all other key variables were statistically insignificant.

By harvesting and analyzing an abundance of data sets as they pertain to critical topics in American politics, Professor Tate provides an invaluable resource to students and researchers of Black politics. In terms of her central thesis that public opinions follows leadership, the evidence is less convincing.

Tate's theoretical framework builds on Adolph Reed's notion that the Black community has witnessed a shift from leaders with activist backgrounds to leaders who have spent the bulk of their careers in political office. Another part of her framework draws on Robert Michel's theory of political parties, which views them as moderate forms of representation and political action. She draws these strands together to argue that today's Black leadership class is less ideologically radical and their inclusion has led to a moderating influence in Black politics. Many scholars of Black politics have sought to analyze the evolving ideological and leadership shifts in the post Civil Rights context, employing concepts like systemic and non-systemic politics, inclusionary versus non-inclusionary, and deracialization in attempt to understand contemporary Black politics. But Tate is one of the first scholars to assert that there is a causal relationship between moderate Black leaders and the moderation of Black public opinion in many areas.

Whether or not one accepts Tate's theoretical premise, as opposed to environmental or socioeconomic positions, is debatable. The main shortcoming of the text is not theoretical, but of a methodological nature. While the author clearly indicates various shifts in Black public opinion, the regression models that she employs in an attempt to prove her thesis are limited in their results and inferential potential. This weakness is partially a result of the methodological decision to use a mix of heterogeneous data sets. In fact, the author acknowledges the methodological limits of the study in the opening chapter. "My thesis is that the changing character of Black political leadership influenced Black public opinion over time, not the other way around. Causal order, however, is best established through experimental design . . . My principle claim that political elites have influenced Black public opinion is based on indirect rather than direct evidence" (12). Unable to draw from an experimental design formatted to the project's objectives, Tate must rely on a non-uniform set of indirect measures from various data sets. When using the NBES studies she uses a broad range of variables measuring both communal dynamics and Black leadership, but when employing the ANES, GSS (General Social Surveys), or media surveys the models include a smaller number of leadership indicators. Data limitations also blur Tate's central thesis, in some of the models leadership is statistically tied to specific leaders or organizations, but in other models leadership is connected to Party ID or ideology. At some points, moreover, it is unclear as to whether the author is arguing that Blacks are following the cues of elites (Black or White) or simply becoming typical Democrats.

Even before the election of President Barack Obama, many students of Black politics wrestled with the consequences and effects of integration in a post-civil rights context. Although analysts continue to highlight the widening disparities in key socioeconomic categories between Blacks and Whites, the type of mass oppositional activities and views associated with the movements of the 1960s are nonexistent today. Professor Tate does an excellent job of aggregating a wealth of public opinion data to demonstrate how Blacks have become more moderate over the past two decades. Though some sociologists or economists may attribute this moderation process to socioeconomic factors, the author empirically highlights how these views are not limited to a particular demographic group. The author also makes a strong case that absent the infusion of radical actors, who have the ability to counter the conservative and centrist frames of the current political leadership, African American public opinion will continue to drift closer to the dominant norms of the Democratic Party on several issues. Overall, the author provides an engaging discussion of trends in Black public opinion over the past few decades and a promising conceptual framework for future research in this area.

D. Osei Robertson
Bowie State University

Reiter, Bernd and Gladys L. Mitchell. *Brazil's New Racial Politics* (Boulder, CO and London: Lynne Rienner Publishers, 2010), $59.95, 251 pp. ISBN: 978-1-58826-666-8 (cloth).

This recent anthology brings together some of the most exciting current scholarship on race and racism in Brazil. Edited by political scientists Bernd Reiter and Gladys Mitchell, *Brazil's New Racial Politics* includes work by sociologists, anthropologists, political scientists, and scholars in the field of communication studies. This book offers readers a broad overview of some of the key issues and debates shaping current discussions of race, racism, and racial discrimination in Brazil, both in the academy and in the larger society. It is especially noteworthy that the book brings together work by Brazilian and U.S.-based scholars, since there is often a lag in learning about or gaining access to work that has been published in Brazil for U.S. scholars and vice versa. This book also features the work of established and emergent Afro-Brazilian scholars, which is also important given the professional marginalization that is often experienced by Blacks in the Brazilian academy.

The interdisciplinary perspectives presented in *Brazil's New Racial Politics* build upon and extend current scholarship on race in Brazil, by exploring the dynamics of anti-racist activism and identity politics in the country during the early twenty-first century. The analyses found in this book are particularly important and timely since they explore how racial ideas and practices have been reconfigured in Brazil over the past decade. Long considered a racial democracy, Brazil's image as a non-racist country came under increasing public scrutiny during the 1990s. The advent of affirmative action policies in university admissions and employment in 2001, served to further challenge Brazilian notions of racial democracy. As the contributors to *New Racial Politics in Brazil* note, the battle to dismantle racist ideologies and practices has continued in new forms during the early twenty-first century.

The book's editors drew inspiration from political scientist Michael Hanchard's anthology, *Racial Politics in Brazil,* which was published in 1999. This earlier volume contained an interdisciplinary collection of essays focusing on Brazilian racial dynamics from the slavery era to the final decades of the twentieth century. Many of the contributors to *Brazil's New Racial Politics* are scholar-activists who have a deep commitment to the fulfillment of democracy and racial equality in Brazil. As the editors note in the book's introduction, current academic discussions about Brazilian society are "more than just scholarly exercises. They are strongly connected to the country's future, leaving no space for disengaged academic exercises or cynicism. None of the contributors are just doing business-as-usual. They are all aware that they are participating in a greater project, where their voices bear the potential to impact the course of Brazil's future" (9).

Part 1 of the book includes chapters by Bernd Reiter, Gladys L. Mitchell, Angela Figueiredo, and Cloves Luiz Pereira Oliveira. Reiter's chapter, "Whiteness as Capital: Constructing Inclusion and Defending Privilege," examines the dynamics of White privilege in the Brazilian context. Reiter provides a new perspective on Brazilian racism, particularly since most social science research has either implicitly or explicitly focused on the marginalization of the Afro-descendant population, rather than on the privileged status of Whiteness and Brazilians of European ancestry. Moreover, since Whiteness Studies has not taken root as a field of academic investigation in Brazil, as it has in the United States, White Brazilian identity has largely been left unexamined and unproblematized in most academic scholarship. Reiter's argument regarding the racialized implications of inclusion and exclusion in Brazil provides researchers with a fruitful starting point for further reflection and inquiry. In her chapter, "Politicizing Blackness: Afro-Brazilian Color Identification and Candidate Preference," Gladys Mitchell examines how Black candidates are perceived by Black voters in the cities of Salvador and São Paulo. Mitchell's innovative research methodology involved the collection of survey data with Afro-Brazilian voters in both cities. Contrary to much of the scholarly literature on voting preferences in Brazil, Mitchell found that individuals who embraced Blackness through self-identification as *preto* or *pardo* (two Portuguese terms for "black") tended to vote for Black political candidates in higher numbers. As Mitchell notes, this likely means that a potential voting block exists among "Black racially conscious Afro-Brazilian voters" (49). Angela Figueiredo's chapter, "Out of Place: The Experience of the Black Middle Class," provides new insights into the lives of middle class Afro-Brazilians in the city of Salvador, Bahia. This chapter makes an important contribution to scholarly understandings of the relationship between race and class in Brazil, particularly as it shapes the experiences of more affluent and socially mobile Afro-Brazilians. Figueiredo's essay complements the chapters by Gladys Mitchell, Keisha-Khan Perry, and Fernando Conceição, which also focus on the city of Salvador. By examining the Black middle class, Figueiredo moves away from the more traditional scholarly focus on lower-income Afro-Brazilians, while also highlighting the contradictions of Salvador's reputation as the most "black" or "African" city in Brazil. Cloves Luiz Pereira Oliveira's chapter examines perceptions of Black political candidates through and examination of the 1996 election of Celso Pitta as the first Black mayor of the city of São Paulo, Brazil's largest city. By focusing on journalistic coverage of Pitta's campaign, Oliveira explores how race shaped perceptions of Pitta despite his efforts to present himself as a deracialized candidate. This analysis is particularly important given the lack of attention given to Pitta's candidacy in most academic scholarship.

In Part 2 of the book, Seth Racusen and Mónica Treviño González examine affirmative action policies in Brazil. While sympathetic to the value of race-based and class-based affirmative action policies, Racusen points out shortcomings of some of the admission policies that have been used by Brazilian universities. His analysis also highlights the potential impact of affirmative action policies for the politics of racial identity and racial self-identification in the country. In her essay, Mónica Treviño González examines university admissions quotas in the state of Rio de Janeiro. González explores the role that White privilege played in shaping opposition to the use of quotas and also examines the ineffectiveness of Black activists in challenging such opposition. Like Racusen's essay, the chapter by González provides important insights into the debate over affirmative action policies in Brazilian higher education and moves the academic discussion about such policies beyond a superficial analysis.

Part 3 of the book includes chapters by Keisha-Khan Y. Perry, Sales Augusto dos Santos, Fernando Conceição, and Renato Emerson dos Santos. Keisha-Khan Perry's chapter, "Racialized History and Urban Politics: Black Women's Wisdom in Grassroots Struggles" explores the gendered aspects of urban policies in the city of Salvador. Unlike many previous scholars, Perry highlights the significance of Black women's grassroots organizing as an important form of struggle for "greater social and economic rights, political recognition, and participation" (2010, 147). The chapter by Sales Augusto dos Santos, "Black NGOs and 'Conscious' Rap: New Agents of the Antiracism Struggle in Brazil," examines the emergence of Black NGOs, most of which have been led by women, and the artists of conscious rap. While recognizing the important shift that took place with the emergence of Black NGOs, Santos also calls attention to the crucial role played by what he terms "traditional" or "classic" Black social movements. Santos also highlights the importance of recognizing and validating multiple forms of anti-racist activism, which is reflected in his use of the term "Black social movements" in the plural. Fernando Conceição's analysis in "Power and Black Organizing in Brazil" serves to further deconstruct the city of Salvador's image as the most "African" or "Black" city in Brazil by exploring the municipal elections of 1985. Conceição notes that the success of Afro-Brazilian cultural groups in the city of Salvador failed to translate into increased access to political power for Afro-Brazilians. The final chapter by Renato Emerson dos Santos, "New Social Activism: University Entry Courses for Black and Poor Students," analyzes the effectiveness of courses that prepare students for the *vestibular* (college entrance exam) with respect to enhanced racial awareness and the racialization process. Santos argues that these courses play an important role in disseminating antiracist activism in the country. This analysis offers an important link to the essays by Racusen and González by demonstrating how preparatory courses can work in tandem with official state policy to deepen debate about race and racism in Brazil.

Given the wide-ranging subject matter covered in *Brazil's New Racial Politics,* this book will be of interest to scholars and students in the fields of political science, sociology, and anthropology, as well as those in African-American/African Diaspora Studies and Latin American and Caribbean Studies. The essays are written in an accessible and informative style which will also make the book suitable for use in a wide-variety of undergraduate and graduate courses, as well as by scholars new to Brazilian studies and established Brazilianists alike.

Kia Lilly Caldwell
University of North Carolina, Chapel Hill

Robinson, Cedric J. *Forgeries of Memory and Meaning: Blacks & the Regimes of Race in American Theater & Film before World War II* (Chapel Hill, NC: University of North Carolina Press, 2007), $24.95, 456 pp. ISBN: 978-0-8078-5841-7 (paper).

In its simplest terms, Cedric J. Robinson's *Forgeries of Memory and Meaning: Blacks & the Regimes of Race in American Theater & Film before World War II* is a history of film, capitalism, and the construction of racial ideology. However, there is little that can be easily simplified about the analysis with which Robinson presents the reader. To understand how it is unique in race and film theory, it is necessary to take account of the framework Robinson adopts constructing this analysis, particularly his conceptualization of race and power, and the way this framework intervenes into and challenges the tendency of scholarship on these topics toward rhetorical overtotalization. First, the idea that race is socially constructed to justify relations of power should be well-known to Robinson's audience, yet his analysis pursues this idea further by exploring: what does it mean for racial regimes to possess history? In such histories suppressed by racial regimes "masquerading as memory and the immutable" (xii) Robinson finds (or rather, recovers) evidence of the agency of the oppressed continually recurring within and exposing the shortcomings of these modes of domination. So the irrationality of racial ideology which makes it an "uncontrollable causative" (29) is also the source of its inherent instability, forcing racial regimes to continually remake themselves. Second, the instability of racial regimes challenges theories of power which eschew its limitations, conflicts, and unintended consequences, particularly with regard to the role of resistance. This is why Robinson sometimes uses the example of fugitive slaves and marronage when elaborating this principle; these dis-remembered traces of human agency showed how those subjected to the most absolute form of domination still imagined and sought out the system's exterior. Also, counterposing the image of fugitivity against his account of development of racial regimes connects it to Robinson's earlier work *Black Marxism: The Making of the Black Radical Tradition*, implicitly establishing a parallel tradition of resistance. Third, the conclusion that "the production of race is chaotic" (xii) is a reflection of his broader view of history, which he similarly characterizes as chaotic. Robinson's historiography is best exemplified in the style of his writing, which is certainly quite dense. While this is at least a credit to his own brilliance—he has the habit of permitting minor aspects of his argument to play out over several pages and of incorporating a diverse range of examples—there is more to Robinson's style than a show of prowess for its own sake. This mode of exposition lays bare the historical record so that the reader feels the weight of these histories of resistance against the so-called immutability of race, and in the reader's skepticism, the contradiction between these two forces must be personally negotiated against the backdrop of race's centuries-long conceit.

Chapter 1 begins with an account of representations of Blacks before the modern era and how the iconography of Black inferiorization took root. He draws from multiple sources to conclude that in pre-modern Europe it was by no means the received wisdom that African peoples were naturally inferior to Europeans. The inception of the inferiorized Negro arose during the Elizabethan period; concomitant with the development of English nationalism, its entry into the international slave trade, and its transition from mercantilism to capitalism. He highlights Shakespeare's *Othello* as both a "direct challenge to the emergent Negrophobia" (16) and as a sign of the stigmatization to come. After the image of Black inferiority is set in motion, Robinson follows its course to the early United States, where an extensive history of slave insurrections, marronage, and abolitionism contended with the exclusionary politics of the Revolutionary period, whole fabrications of yet-enduring Black tropes, and finally the development of scientific racism and a nationalist public culture to disseminate it. Robinson has set out a pattern that will continue throughout his study, a dynamic struggle between diffusion of new racial regimes and their contestation.

Chapter 2 first negotiates criticisms of Donald Bogle's *Toms, Coons, Mulattos, Mammies, & Bucks*. Emphasizing the work of Thomas Cripps, Robinson describes how Black cinematographers challenged the immutable Black cinematic tropes described by Bogle "by contextualizing his icons in particular sociohistorical conflicts" (84). Though Robinson seems to disagree with the inflexibility of Bogle's typology, he does assent that minstrelsy tends to recur throughout the history of American film. To settle the matter, he takes a detour through an example regarding Marx. He compares Marx's inability to understand the appeal of Ancient Greek culture for his society to Cripps's puzzlement over the causes of the introduction of negative Black stereotypes in early American cinema. The key point that these two were missing, Robinson argues, is the ability for cultural signifiers to be carried beyond their original purpose and social context. Therefore, the introduction of negative Black stereotypes into film was both a continuation and reassertion of previous forms of racialization. Yet, the period of American film inaugurated by Griffith's, *The Birth of a Nation,* (1915) distinguished itself by elaborating what Ed Guerrero calls the "plantation genre." In contrast to the social context of the early national period, cinema and the racial order now colluded to meet the needs of "a robust industrial society voraciously appropriating a vast but disparate labor force which required cultural discipline, social habituation, and political regulation" (92). This was achieved by distorting the history of slavery and reinscribing racial hierarchy into the social imaginary. Specifically, aspects of slavery such as race mixture, rape of female slaves, resistance from both slaves and White labor, and abolitionism were effaced. These remaining portrayals only had space for plantocrats, sub-human Blacks, and infantilized White Southern aristocratic women. The result of this erasure, Robinson recounts, was "a new, virile American whiteness" (108).

Chapter 3 elaborates the history of Blackface minstrelsy, Black minstrelsy, and later Black dramatic theatre. It explains that though Blackface minstrelsy in the early United States has been connected to Irish and German immigrant communities, their ambiguous racial position and shared class position with Black laborers complicate the history of early Blackface minstrelsy. However, an eventual cooption of the genre by middle and upper class Whites traded the class antagonism for pure racial denigration, and was subsequently challenged by the "concealed resistances, gestures of opposition," (130) and alternative histories of Black minstrelsy. Robinson focuses in on the instructive example of the *mulatta* and the Black chorus girl to exemplify both how the exhibition of their desirability and theatrical talent could be used to disrupt negative Black images, yet still find itself within the ideological terms those images have constructed. Finally, he describes the continuation of these traditions of resistance in Black dramatic theatre, yet despite these efforts, Robinson does not ignore how the continual struggle to foreground the ruptures and contradictions in the anti-Black representations was made an uphill battle by unequal power relations. Yet for the purposes of his argument, I believe the necessary gesture here is to recognize the artifact of human agency which Robinson has recovered.

In contrast to accounts of the beginnings of the American film industry which characterize it as haphazard, Robinson problematizes the concurrence of Jim Crow segregation and the inception of motion pictures as a mass media. In fact, Robinson argues that this coincidence illustrates why images of Black inferiorization migrated into the medium. As we have seen before, the instability of racial regimes demands that they are continually re-forged, and likewise, the ideological apparatus which justifies them must be reimagined. With regard to this period, Robinson states that "apartheid was the structural instrument of American capital, and American filmmakers supplied a galaxy of imagery and story lines which naturalized and popularized white hegemony" (201). Chapter 4 also deals with the ways in which independent Black cinema developed resistances to this flood of denigration, though the success of the response is itself complex. He opens the question of how to characterize the genre known at the time as "race films," not merely because the body of work had a mixed relationship with regard to negative Black images, but also because Robinson is hard pressed to find any filmic conventions adopted by this alternative cinema. Furthermore, though a number of such race films introduced contesting iconography through positive images of Black life, such as those which featured any portrayal of the Black middle class whatsoever, Robinson finds that ". . . the best of race films fell short of Lott's call for a cinema which confronted 'the oppressive and self-destructive consciousness the empire seeks to perpetuate'" (241). The only exception he identifies is the work of Oscar Micheaux. This chapter closes with an extensive analysis of Micheaux's *Within Our Gates* (1920); focusing on the structural elements of jazz within the film, its refutation of Black inferiorization broadly, and Griffith's racism specifically, and its transition from melodrama to social drama. This last aspect of *Within Our Gates* is achieved through ruptures in the film's text, such that the interpersonal conflicts of the erstwhile melodrama are eventually submerged under the weight of racial oppression and conspiracy. Ultimately, the breach of the closed melodrama with social critique parallels the film's rupture of the "closed texts of racism" (207) which plagued contemporaneous films in mainstream cinema.

Chapter 5 describes how the beginning of the sound era continued and refined the impersonation of Blacks and Black music. He focuses in on how the films *Hearts in Dixie* (1929) and *Hallelujah* (1929) constructed a myth of the innate poverty of African Americans through a deliberate omission of the social conditions which produced this mass dispossession, i.e., peonage. Then broadening his analysis, he contextualizes this so-called "Golden Age" of Hollywood cinema within the sociopolitical trends of the time; drawing the connection in dense detail between the massive expansion of imperialist capitalism and the erection of yet another facet of cinematic racial propaganda: the jungle film genre. This genre, which Robinson considers complementary to Guerrero's plantation genre, continues to perpetuate the erasure of African histories, civilizations, and humanity but adds to the fray colonialist ideas and images. The remainder of this last chapter describes the all-Black-cast film and Black independent cinema as a growing site of resistance, especially the work of Mantan Moreland; who despite costuming his performances in familiar trappings of minstrelsy, managed to create a comedic space of commentary, critique, and inversion.

It is interesting, though, that Robinson should end an analysis so marked by cyclical change once again in a moment of rupture. Though this most likely follows from his sources and the boundaries of his study, I like to think that this is meant to reaffirm the perennial challenge this text poses against racism's "regime of truth." As the reader follows this history, which is often fraught with injustice, to its open conclusion, it becomes clear that though Robinson's framework serves him well as an analytical framework, it also forms the basis for a call to action. In the end, despite learning the history of how, through beguilement and counterfeiture, these racial regimes have long outlived their time, the reader is rewarded with the impression that their collapse can occur at any moment.

Michael Tran
University of Oregon

Hunt, Darnell and Ana-Christina Ramon, eds. *Black Los Angeles: American Dreams and Racial Realities* (New York: New York University Press, 2010), $26.00, 432 pp. ISBN: 0-8147-3735-8 (paper).

Black Los Angeles: American Dreams and Racial Realities is the culmination of a series of workshops held over the course of eight years at the Ralph J. Bunche Center for African American Studies at UCLA. The Black Los Angeles project, as it was initially named, brought together scholars and community members to describe and define the concrete existence of a significant population of the southern California metropolis whose reality for most of America, and possibly the world, has been filtered largely through the fiction of movies and television. According to Darnell Hunt, Director of the Bunche Center and Professor of Sociology at UCLA, "it is an attempt to connect the dots between the past, present and future of a space that was seeded centuries ago with a profound black presence, that has attracted hundreds of thousands of black migrants in the intervening years, but that oddly enough, is only marginally understood as a black place." (Hunt 2–3).

The mission of the contributors to this edition, was to put into context the lives and the morphing communities of Los Angeles's Black metropolis. For the purpose of analysis Black Los Angeles was strategically separated into five central themes (communities and neighborhoods, religious life, political participation, cultural production, and social justice) organized into four sections: *Space, People, Image,* and *Action*. The essays that comprise the sixteen chapters are admirable in their scope and illuminating in their examination of the American dream versus African American realities in the quintessential land of make believe.

In Chapter 1, Paul Robinson takes on the issue of space and right of place in his article titled, *Race, Space, and the Evolution of Black Los Angeles* by informing the reader of the city's founding fathers and mothers who shared an African ancestry. Robinson reminds us that while Thomas Bradley was widely hailed in 1973 as the first Black mayor of LA, a more thorough reading will reveal that Francisco Reyes preceded him by at least 200 years. Throughout the 1970s and 1980s Los Angeles street gangs gained notoriety both as real purveyors of genocidal homicide and fictional fodder for endless law and order television dramas. In Chapter 5 *Out of the Void: Street Gangs in Los Angeles*, Alex Alonso addresses the issue of how racial discrimination in both systemic and systematic employment and housing discrimination conspired to create an environment that was an ideal incubator for the birth and proliferation of gangs like the Bloods, the Crips, and many others. Many years before the development of these pathological entities, Black Angelenos were the envy of African American communities across the nation. Soon after their emergence in the late nineteenth century as California's largest African American population they attracted the attention of African American leaders such as Booker T. Washington,

Marcus Garvey, and W.E.B. Dubois for their economic and political acumen. In Chapter 13, Melina Abdullah and Regina Freer introduce the reader to one extremely influential Black Angeleno, of which far too little is known, while acknowledging her legacy in *Bass to Bass: Relative Freedom and Womanist Leadership in Black Los Angeles.*

In the mid-1970s, Los Angeles became my home after transferring to attend UCLA. Until then my knowledge and disdain of southern California was biased by my tenure as a long-term resident of northern California—Beat LA! However, one should never judge a book by its cover. Over the next quarter century, as both a citizen and curator of history at the California African American Museum, my love and appreciation for the City of the Angels, its vibrant African American community, and I matured accordingly. The history of Black Los Angeles is a history that perhaps reads best over time, and especially when the time is taken to savor it. But, even if you are short on time, I nevertheless recommend an immersion into *Black Los Angeles: American Dreams and Racial Realities*. Darnell Hunt and Ana-Christina Ramon provide the reader with a vintage product that is well worth tasting.

Rick Moss
African American Museum & Library at Oakland

McCarthy, Thomas. *Race, Empire, and the Idea of Human Development* (New York: Cambridge University Press, 2009), $29.99, 262 pp. ISBN: 978-0-521-74043-2 (cloth).

Thomas McCarthy's book, *Race, Empire, and the Idea of Human Development*, represents an attempt to propose a critical theory of development, which locates racism and imperialism at the crux of ideas of development rather than its unfortunate ugly stepchildren. To this end, McCarthy engages in a process of deconstruction and reconstruction of the unlikely compatibility of liberal universalism and apologetics for racism and imperialism via a sweeping exploration of Kant's philosophy of history, the roots of scientific racism, the politics of memory of American slavery, and contemporary forms of neoliberal and neoconservative globalization. McCarthy's contribution comes in the form of a synthesis of Habermas' discourse ethics, Kantian cosmopolitanism, multicultural pluralism, and Rawlsian liberalism. Out of this, McCarthy fashions a theoretical way out of the "glittering misery" of the civilized state and a position between pragmatic conservatism on the right and the various postcolonial, feminist, and anti-racist contingencies on the left. Despite McCarthy's good intentions (What's that saying about good intentions?) to resuscitate Kantian Enlightenment ideas of development and cobble together a progressive concept of global development free of imperialist and racist ideology, ultimately, he falls prey to overgeneralization and fails to adequately delineate his object of inquiry and sort through the disparate logics that underpin these ideas and movements to discern the emancipatory wheat from the reactionary chaff.

For example, in McCarthy's discussion of the rise, fall, and makeover of social Darwinism, he explains that where biology was shown inadequate to provide links between phenotype and character, the links were instead "forged historically in various systems of racial oppression, adaptation to which by those oppressed gave rise to 'cultural pathologies' of various sorts." McCarthy argues that although "natural-scientific" versions of racist discourse have been banished from official discourses of the academy and the state they have found new homes within the social-science discourses of underdevelopment. The structures of neo-racist ideology underpinning current developmental schemas of history have been obscured to the point of non-existence leaving only the sanitized pathological explanations of oppressed groups in terms of what McCarthy calls the "racialized grammars of difference." These grammars are then used to explain social structure and processes (while at the same time contributing to the calcification of the associations) rather than to understand their reciprocal nature. For me, that's a little too vague.

McCarthy's argument would have been made stronger had he more concretely illuminated how these explanations map raced bodies and racially inflected inequalities along a developmental continuum based on things such as poverty, social, and/or cultural dysfunction and deprivation from which psychological and cultural associations are made. (Think *Moynihan Report* and benign neglect.) Where I find some of McCarthy's most interesting and insightful analysis is in his chapter, "On the politics of the memory of slavery." In this chapter, McCarthy does a better job at making explicit the process by which the racist foundations of the United States are absorbed into a developmental schema and recast within the master narrative of the state as regional "aberrations" or traumatic hiccups in an otherwise natural developmental process.

What McCarthy fails to examine however is that ultimately, all of the above are critical consequences of the problematic and fundamental exclusions haunting the peripheries of Enlightenment ideas of human development. Use, abuse, and misuse, of developmental schemas of representation have allowed (to a certain degree) the unexamined continuation of post-biological racism and post-colonial imperialism. It is these mutated pathological forms that present themselves as compatible with formal ideals of independence, equality, and freedom. Attending to such details would seem important to his stated project. To miss these points ignores the means by which neoconservatives have been able to commandeer the metaphors and rhetoric of universalism, freedom, and democracy while neoliberals have found themselves in the embrace of reactionary defenses of non-Western relativism and status quos. These are the deeper processes we ought to be questioning, and new syntheses or reformulations of Enlightenment ideas cannot help illuminate this present darkness precisely because they are *part of its origins*.

If part of McCarthy's project was to engage Kant's question "What may I hope?" he offers a tepid and admittedly melancholic answer. McCarthy states "while the contingency of history make utopian hopes—and, of course, dystopian fears—*possible* in principle, we are concerned here with what is *reasonable* to hope for and work towards, in light of what we know about past history and present circumstances . . ." (238). How dreary and status quo. His concluding chapter continually stresses "practical" points of view and in this respect, McCarthy's argument is no different from the neo-liberal bias toward the politically "reasonable" and sadly highlights how (particularly for those originally excluded from modernity) too often what may be hoped for is compromised by "present circumstances." Can't we do better than that?

Sherri Taylor
The Wright Institute

Winkle-Wagner, Rachelle. *The Unchosen Me: Race, Gender, and Identity Among Black Women in College* (Baltimore, MD: The Johns Hopkins University Press, 2009), $57.00, 248 pp. ISBN: 978-0-80189-354-4 (cloth).

In *The Unchosen Me: Race, Gender, and Identity Among Black Women in College*, Rachelle Winkle-Wagner presents her findings from a qualitative research study in which she documents the experiences of thirty Black college women attending a predominately White institution (PWI) in the Midwest. Winkle-Wagner takes a sociological approach to explore racialized and gendered aspects of identity development among these women. She borrows from W. E. B. DuBois's *double consciousness* and more recently, Jones and Shorter-Gooden's *shifting* (2003) concepts to describe a "two-ness" Black people often negotiate living in America. Specific to higher education, these concepts refer to the perception of what it means to be a "good Black woman," against the backdrop of what it means to be successful at an institution of higher learning. She concludes that these women are left with an "unchosen me," a forced identity necessary to gain success, recognition, and access to economic and social mobility. Based on her findings, Winkle-Wagner takes a social justice approach and challenges college administrators to critically examine ways in which campus climates impose identities on students, and to ask what identities are privileged on campus, what identities are outright rejected, and what identities are left invisible. Winkle-Wagner should be commended for her contribution to the literature and for expanding the discussion of what college administrators can do to positively affect the retention of African American women.

In Chapters 4–7, Winkle-Wagner begins presenting her detailed findings. She documents the college experiences of Brandi, Ariel, Isis, Krystal, Camille, Maya, and twenty-four other Black women who attended a PWI in the Midwest. In these chapters, the women become more than data points as Winkle-Wagner quotes them extensively and draws interconnections among their stories. She notes identity struggles related to feelings of being invisible versus being in the spotlight, of culture shock and a sense of loneliness, of being "too black or not black enough." Winkle-Wagner argues that the identities which these women choose are highly influenced by their perceptions of who they need to be in order to be successful. She argues that an imposed identity negatively affects retention, students' sense of belonging and subsequent involvement on campus, and academic performance.

Winkle-Wagner concludes with an analysis of the implications directed toward college administrators and higher education policy makers. She charges administrators to increase support structures for African American students and to incorporate them "into the mainstream of campus rather than on the fringes" (158). She encourages administrators to provide the space for frequent, positive, and affirming interracial contact and interaction between students, faculty, and staff across the campus. Specific examples include policies related to the manner in which students are selected for honors programs, how students are placed in certain residence halls, times, and locations of campus events, and the management of their financial responsibilities.

As with any study, there are growth edges and considerations for future research. In Chapter 1, Winkle-Wagner compares and contrasts psychological versus sociological approaches to studying identity. She critiques psychological models of identity development asserting that because they begin with the study of the "individual single self . . . [there is] little room for the consideration about the impact of the social structure, inequality, or discrimination on identity development" (15). She specifically cites Cross's 1995 model of Nigrescence as an example and highlights assumptions of the model's linear design. She concludes that this model, and others like it do not explain multiple identities and the, "acclimation to multiple situations and contexts" (16). However, while Cross's 1995 model is not without critique, more recent developments to Black racial identity models enlarge the initial model and dispel misconceptions that there is inherent value assigned to distinct and static stages (Cross and Vandiver 2001; Vandiver et al. 2001). Furthermore, Winkle-Wagner ignores an entire flood in psychological research that addresses issues of multiple identities, and the interaction of these identities often referred to as intersectionality (Abes et al. 2007; Cole 2009; Levin et al 2002; Oksana et al. 2009).

Winkle-Wagner argues that in the sociological approach to understanding identity development, "society develops first and then one's self initiates within that society" (17). It is within this context that Winkle-Wagner finds an avenue to explore "the way social inequality . . . may influence students while they are in college, placing the primary responsibility for inequality squarely on the social structure rather than the individual" (17). While I agree that the sociological approach is appropriate for this particular study, I believe Winkle-Wagner misses the mark by not highlighting the strengths of the psychological approach. By nature, psychology is the study of the person, and their interactions within a given environment. This individual approach can be empowering and information gained through this type of research can help Black college students learn to empower themselves as they navigate an unjust and unequal society. On the other hand, by nature, sociology is the study of the environment. Theories based out of this perspective are charged with the task of affecting policy and law that dictate social norms, and create climate. In conjunction with the psychological approach (not in opposition to), the outcome could be more interesting.

When Winkle-Wagner discloses her own identity as a White woman conducting this study, she acknowledges the challenges she faces and some of the possible limitations of her research. However, these are limitations that have been well documented on researcher's bias related to race (Mizock et al. 2011; Sherman 2002; Thompson et al. 1994; Whaley 2001). It would be interesting to discern how the narratives would read differently if the facilitator were African American.

In summary, Winkle-Wagner presents a detailed account of the impact the college environment has on the racial and gender identity development of young Black college women. She highlights ways in which these students are often forced to adopt certain attributes if they want to gain recognition in a university environment. Her work should be commended for naming this dynamic as unjust and for attributing the responsibility for correcting this injustice to the institutions themselves.

References

Abes, E.S., Jones, S.R. & McEwen, M.K. (2007). Reconceptualizing the Model of Multiple Dimensions of Identity: The Role of Meaning-Making Capacity in the Construction of Multiple Identities. *Journal of College Student Development 48*(1), 1–22.

Cole, E. R. (2009). Intersectionality and research in psychology. *American Psychologist, 64*(3), 170–80.

Cross, W. E., Jr. (1995). The psychology of nigrescence: Revising the Cross model. In J. G. Ponterotto, J. M. Casas, L. A. Suzuki, & C. M. Alexander (Eds.), *Handbook of multicultural counseling* (pp. 93–122). Thousand Oaks, CA: Sage.

Cross, W. E., Jr., & Vandiver, B. J. (2001). Nigrescence theory and measurement: Introducing the Cross Racial Identity Scale (CRIS). In J. G. Ponterotto, J. M. Casas, L. A. Suzuki, & C. M. Alexander (Eds.), *Handbook of multicultural counseling* (2nd ed., pp. 371–93). Thousand Oaks, CA: Sage.

Levin, S., Sinclair, S., Veniegas, R. & Taylor, P. (2002). Perceived discrimination in the context of multiple social identities. *Psychological Science, 13*, 557–60.

Mizock, L., Harkins, D. & Morant, R. (2011). Researcher Interjecting in Qualitative Race Research. *Qualitative Social Research, 12*(2), Art. 13, http://nbn-resolving.de/urn:nbn:de:0114-fqs1102134.

Oksana, Y., Davidson, M. M. & Williams, E.N. (2009). Identity salience model: A paradigm for integrating multiple identities in clinical practice. *Psychotherapy: Theory, Research, Practice, Training, 46*(2), 180–92.

Sherman, Richard (2002). The subjective experience of race and gender in qualitative research. *American Behavioral Scientist, 45*(8), 1247–53.

Thompson, C. E., Worthington, R. & Atkinson, D. R. (1994). Counselor content orientation, counselor race, and Black women's cultural mistrust and self-disclosures. *Journal of Counseling Psychology, 41*(2), 155–61.

Vandiver, B.J., Fhagen-Smith, P.E., Cokley, K.O & Cross, W.E., Jr. (2001). Cross's nigrescence model: From theory to scale to theory. *Journal of Multicultural Counseling and Development, 29*(3).

Whaley, A.L. (2001). Cultural mistrust and mental health services for African Americans: A review and meta-analysis. *The Counseling Psychologist, 29*(5), 515–31.

Taisha Caldwell
University of California, Irvine

McClain, Paula D. and Steven C. Tauber. *American Government in Black and White* (Boulder, CO: Paradigm Publishers, 2010), $67.11, 544 pp. ISBN: 978-1-59451-497-5 (paper).

American Government in Black and White covers topics that one would study in any introduction to American government courses. Chapters focus on fundamentals such as the Constitution, civil liberties, the three branches of government, and the policy-making process. What distinguishes this text is its consistent focus on the ways that the construct of race has influenced American government. Rather than treating race as an incidental factor that has influenced America's political structures and systems, McClain and Tauber intentionally center their analysis around it, arguing that an individual cannot gain an accurate understanding of American government without investigating the ways that race has affected the development of our political system.

A focus on critical civic and community engagement creates an interesting platform for considering the contributions of this text. Civic and community engagement involves community building at all levels—from overtly political activities to informal relationship building among community members. It therefore serves the larger purposes of political science and higher education for a textbook to address issues in a way that encourages readers to become more involved citizens. When community building activities are performed with a recognition of the fundamental power imbalances and other systemic challenges that are embedded in our societies, civic and community engagement becomes critical in nature. With that in mind, this book review is meant to consider what *American Government in Black and White* has to offer in terms of facilitating and encouraging civic and community engagement and helping develop the critical consciousness of readers.

The text lays out its fundamental argument early on, asserting that any analysis of American government and politics must take race into account. The rationale is that readers of all races should understand that issues of race have endured throughout America's history and affected all of its citizens. The authors begin with an examination of what they characterize as "America's long and painful struggle with race from the time of Thomas Jefferson, a slave owner, to President Barak Obama, the first Black president of the United States" (xvii). McClain and Tauber articulate the worry of many Black Americans that Barak Obama's election to the Presidency would be interpreted by some as a sign that race is no longer a core aspect of the U.S. political landscape. In theory, if Obama's election means structural, systematic racism is no longer an issue, this leaves only individualistic explanations for societal inequalities. Such a conclusion may in turn be used to further arguments that anti-discrimination policies are no longer necessary.

The authors assert that Obama's race may indeed make it more difficult to address issues of racial inequality because his election allowed many Americans to conclude that issues of racism, discrimination, and oppression have been resolved. However, the reality is, in order to be elected, Obama did not focus on issues of special importance to Black Americans. While his election does demonstrate a certain level of success due to the perseverance and talents of Blacks, we must remember that any forward movement in this country has always been threatened by backlash. Obama's election therefore makes it even more necessary to identify and eradicate the pervasiveness of racial discrimination in the United States in order to secure conditions that allow for the success of all Americans, not just an extraordinary few.

The book is written in a way that engages readers by approaching common topics in American government from a race-conscious point of view. This move creates the intellectual space to progress beyond the rhetoric of American politics in order to recognize the ways that racial discrimination has shaped the functioning of our government. Though this may be uncomfortable for some, using the text in this way can inform contemporary readers, helping them see areas where significant progress has been made as well as areas where more work must be done to make American government serve all of its citizens. While the book does move in this direction, it does not explicitly encourage any form of engagement with the political system. Instead, it stops at illuminating disjunctures between the theory and practice of American government.

Like McClain's other text, *Can We All Get Along*, McClain and Tauber structure their book around dilemmas underlying America's political system. The key dilemma relates to how government reconciles the tension between stated principles of equality and actual governmental practices toward individuals and groups representing different races. For example, after reviewing state and federal apologies for slavery and Jim Crow along with a brief mention of other apologies, the government has issued to Japanese Americans and Hawaiians, the text asks a series of questions which explore the rhetoric of equality versus the reality of America's unequal treatment of many. The questions include, "Why did a government founded on the concepts of freedom and equality engage in actions and put in place policies that were inequitable and unjust? Why is it so difficult for this government to make amends for the inequities and inequalities it created? Who benefits from inequalities? Is it possible to correct inequalities for those aggrieved without creating the belief that the government is reducing opportunities for others" (3)?

These questions can be used to stimulate critical thinking among readers by problematizing the inequalities that many American government texts gloss over and taking up the question of what types of social action have taken place and could take place in order to bring America closer to the country's stated ideals. These are exactly the kinds of questions that critical civic and community engagement is meant to address. Although the text does not provide information regarding the possibilities for readers to engage their government and address these contradictions, it does create a space for motivated students to consider forms of critical engagement on their own.

Later in the text, the authors' framework for the foundations of American government serves as a key feature. The text covers classical liberalism (freedom of individual and government responsibility to protect that freedom); republicanism (belief that democratic rule should be indirect); and inegalitarianism (tradition of excluding large segments of the population from political participation) as three of the key foundations of American government (8). This book does not treat the inegalitarian conditions created and perpetuated by the American government as anomalies in America's historical experience. Instead, inegalitarianism is solidly framed as a tradition upon which the U.S. government is based, making it a central issue which any student of American government must reckon with. McClain and Tauber make a potentially important move here by identifying exclusion as an American tradition because it allows them to identify specific acts throughout the history of American government as examples of this tradition. However, the authors do not refer back to this foundation of American government in subsequent parts of the text.

Continuing the discussion of American inegalitarianism could help readers identify ways that this tradition has endured in contemporary life. It would also help provide readers with the tools to interrogate the practices of American government and move communities forward by challenging practices that continue to support inequality and discrimination. When facilitating critical civic and community engagement, these facts are important because they help readers understand that many of their rights of political participation have evolved slowly, and they are continuously challenged. One potential goldmine for engagement lies in the text's special sections.

Each chapter contains special informational boxes, which are meant to make abstract ideas seem more real for readers. Vignettes in the text highlight complex inequalities through stories drawn from actual events. The figures and tables add to the book's empirical basis while also recognizing readers' different learning styles. The "Measuring Equality," "Our Voices," and "Evaluating Equality" sections encourage critical thinking and interrogation of important issues in American government. These sections are useful for helping readers investigate big ideas by breaking them down into key issues and topics that readers are more likely to identify with. It would be ideal if these boxes also asked readers to consider how the issues covered in the text apply to their own experience, thereby priming them for critical engagement as they begin to think about how they can act to address that concern them.

America in Black and White does a good job of expressing an expectation that readers think critically about American government and politics. It treats the dilemmas of American government as problems to be interrogated rather than simply accepted. It is an important first step for an American government text to systematically examine how race has been an enduring aspect of America's political fabric. It would be a welcome addition if the text also engaged readers in the process of viewing themselves as political actors, capable of impacting American government around social issues they care about.

While the text strongly supports critical thinking around issues of race, it leads me to wonder about other intersectional issues, including class, gender, sexuality, ability, and other historical bases for discrimination. The text draws the reader in because of its willingness to acknowledge the complexities created when race and racial discrimination influence American government and politics. Certainly, it is a daunting task, but perhaps subsequent editions of the text will expand readers' understandings of American government even further by exploring all of these dimensions. Until then, *American Government in Black and White* represents a step in the right direction.

Zahra Ahmed
University of California, Irvine

The National Political Science Review (NPSR)
Invitation to the Scholarly Community

The editors of *The National Political Science Review* (NPSR) invite submissions from the scholarly community for review and possible publication.

The NPSR is a refereed journal of the National Conference of Black Political Scientists. Its editions appear annually and comprise the highest quality scholarship related to the experiences of African Americans in the American political community as well as in the wider reach of the African diaspora in the Western Hemisphere. It also focuses on the international links between African Americans and the larger community of nations, particularly with Africa.

Among the more common areas of research which the NPSR considers for publication are those typically associated with political behavior and attitudes, the performance of political institutions, the efficacy of public policy, interest groups and social movements, inter-ethnic coalition building, and theoretical reflections which offer insights on the minority political experience. Based on recent interest, the NPSR also considers work on the role of culture in politics.

Manuscripts should be submitted in the following format. Submissions should follow the style conventions of the *American Political Science Review* (APSR), and sent to the editors in Microsoft Word format. Two copies of the submissions should be conveyed electronically to the editors at the email addresses listed below. One copy of the submission should include author's or authors' information comprising of the name that will appear in the published version along with the author's/authors' institutional affiliation and email addresses. The other copy should delete the author's/authors' information from the title page. Please indicate the lead author and email address in cases of multiple authors. Manuscripts should not carry footnotes at the bottom of the page. Manuscripts should not exceed thirty (30) typewritten pages, double spaced, inclusive of notes and references, and should be prepared and sent to the editors in Microsoft Word format.

Manuscripts are reviewed on a rolling basis. However, submissions should be received no later than June 15 of the current year to be considered for publication in a forthcoming issue.

Further queries about the NPSR as well as submissions may be addressed (email only) to the editors at:

Michael Mitchell
Co-Editor of the NPSR
School of Politics and Global Studies
Arizona State University
email: michael.mitchell@asu.edu

David Covin, Co-Editor of the NPSR
Government Department (Emeritus)
California State University-Sacramento
email: covindl@csus.edu

For Product Safety Concerns and Information please contact our EU
representative GPSR@taylorandfrancis.com
Taylor & Francis Verlag GmbH, Kaufingerstraße 24, 80331 München, Germany

www.ingramcontent.com/pod-product-compliance
Lightning Source LLC
Chambersburg PA
CBHW081436270326
41932CB00019B/3226